WORDS
OF
WISDOM

Other similar titles from
Random House Value Publishing, Inc.:

Quotations to Cheer You Up
The Little Book of Values
Life Meditations
Good Advice

WORDS
OF
WISDOM

GRAMERCY BOOKS
NEW YORK

This 1998 edition is published by Gramercy Books, an imprint of
Random House Value Publishing, Inc., by arrangement with
Philanthropic Service for Institutions, Adventist World Headquarters,
12501 Old Columbia Pike, Silver Spring, MD 20904.

Gramercy Books and colophon are trademarks of
Random House Value Publishing, Inc.

Random House
New York • London • Toronto • Sydney • Auckland
http://www.randomhouse.com/

Printed in the United States of America

Library of Congress Cataloging–in–Publication Data

Words of wisdom.
p.   cm.
"Originally published as
Words of Wisdom, for Writers, Speakers & Leaders" —T.p. verso.
Includes index.
ISBN 0–517–18837–6
1. Conduct of life—Quotations, maxims, etc. 2. Quotations,
English.   I. Title.
PN6084.C556W65   1997

808.88'2—dc21   97–27888
                                                                          CIP

CONTENTS

WORDS
OF
WISDOM

APPRECIATION

**Admiration • Awareness • Responsiveness
Gratefulness • Gratitude • Thankfulness**

Gratitude is the sign of noble souls. —*Aesop (620–560 B.C.)*

A word of appreciation often can accomplish what nothing else could accomplish.
—*B.C. Forbes (1880–1954)*

A nation which forgets its defenders will itself be forgotten. —*Calvin Coolidge (1872–1933)*

I have never seen a man who could do real work except under the stimulus of encouragement and enthusiasm and the approval of the people for whom he is working. —*Charles M. Schwab (1862–1939)*

We seldom find people ungrateful as long as we are in a position to be helpful.
—*Francois de la Rochefoucauld (1613–1680)*

Recognition is the greatest motivator. —*Gerard C. Ekedal (1925-)*

Gratitude is the fairest blossom which springs from the soul. —*Henry Ward Beecher (1813–1887)*

Those who are peacemakers will plant seeds of peace and reap a harvest of goodness.— *James 3:18 (LB)*

Praise, of all things, is the most powerful excitement to commendable actions, and animates us in our enterprise. —*Jean de la Bruyere (1645–1696)*

Every community needs a great many communal services. . . . By rewarding such work with honor and esteem, the very best men can be had for nothing. —*John Kenneth Galbraith (1908-)*

The question is not what a man can scorn, or disparage, or find fault with, but what he can love, and value, and appreciate. —*John Ruskin (1819–1900)*

There is as much greatness of mind in acknowledging a good turn, as in doing it.
—*Lucius Annaeus Seneca (4 B.C.– A.D.65)*

Gratitude is not only the greatest of virtues, but the parent of all others.
—*Marcus Tullius Cicero (106–43 B.C.)*

Appreciation can make a day—even change a life. Your willingness to put it into words is all that is necessary.
—*Margaret Cousins (1905-)*

I will smile at friend and foe alike and make every effort to find, in him or her, a quality to praise, now that I realize that the deepest yearning of human nature is the craving to be appreciated.
—*Og Mandino (1923-)*

A great deal of good can be done in the world if one is not too careful who gets the credit.
—*Old Jesuit Motto*

He who receives a good turn should never forget it; he who does one should never remember it. He who receives a benefit should never forget it; he who bestows it should never remember it.
—*Pierre Charron (1541–1603)*

The art of acceptance is the art of making someone who has just done you a small favor wish that he might have done you a greater one.
—*Russell Lynes (1910-)*

To be of value, expressions of appreciation must be continually renewed. —*Sheree Parris Nudd (1954-)*

Three words of praise will soften anybody's heart. —*T. C. Lai (1921-)*

A pat on the back, though only a few vertebrae removed from a kick in the pants, is miles ahead in results.
—*Unknown*

There is more hunger for love and appreciation in this world than for bread. —*Unknown*

There's no doubt about it, appreciation in any form at any time brightens anyone's existence. And, like a beam of sunlight striking a mirror, the brightness is reflected back at you. —*Unknown*

By appreciation we make excellence in others our own property. —*Voltaire (1694–1778)*

Appreciation is a wonderful thing; it makes what is excellent in others belong to us as well.
—*Voltaire (1694–1778)*

If you give appreciation to people, you win their goodwill. But more important than that, practicing this philosophy has made a different person of me.— *William James (1842–1910)*

The deepest principle in human nature is the craving to be appreciated. —*William James (1842–1910)*

BENEVOLENCE

Altruism • Beneficence • Grace
Mercy • Good Will

I want it said of me by those who knew me best that I always plucked a thistle and planted a flower where I thought a flower would grow. —*Abraham Lincoln (1809–1865)*

Seek always to do some good somewhere. You must give some time to your fellow man. For remember, you don't live in a world all your own. —*Albert Schweitzer (1875–1965)*

The monument of a great man is not of granite or marble or bronze. It consists of his goodness, his deeds, his love and his compassion. —*Alfred A. Montapert (1906-)*

I still believe that people are good at heart. —*Anne Frank (1929–1945)*

I just want to leave the world a little better than I found it, and that's my goal in life. —*Armand Hammer (1898–1990)*

Give in to goodness now and then. —*Arthur Gordon (1912-)*

There are glimpses of heaven to us in every act, or thought, or word that raises us above ourselves. —*Arthur P. Stanley (1815–1881)*

I Resolve: to strive to contribute something to the world, its work and the people in it; to spend and be spent in worthy service; to adhere, the best I can, to the Golden Rule. —*B. C. Forbes (1880–1954)*

If your heart is in the right place, it affords you appropriate opportunity to do things for others, to express your good will, to let yourself go sentimentally, philanthropically. —*B. C. Forbes (1880–1954)*

No man who continues to add something to the material, intellectual and moral well-being of the place in which he lives, is left long without proper reward. —*Booker T. Washington (1856–1915)*

Little progress can be made by merely attempting to repress what is evil. Our great hope lies in developing what is good. —*Calvin Coolidge (1872–1933)*

Man cannot really improve himself without improving others. —*Charles Dickens (1812–1870)*

Mankind was my business; charity, mercy, forbearance, and benevolence were all my business. The dealings of my trade were but a drop of water in the comprehensive ocean of my business.
—*Jacob Marley to Ebenezer Scrooge in "A Christmas Carol," Charles Dickens (1812–1870)*

The greatest pleasure I know is to do a good action by stealth, and to have it found out by accident.
—*Charles Lamb (1775–1834)*

One more good man on earth is better than an extra angel in heaven. —*Chinese Proverb*

In the final analysis there is no other solution to man's progress but the day's honest work, the day's honest decision, the day's generous utterances and the day's good deed.
—*Clare Booth Luce (1903–1983)*

He who wishes to secure the good of others has already secured his own. —*Confucius (551–479 B.C.)*

Goodness is something so simple; always live for others, never to seek one's own advantage.
—*Dag Hammarskjold (1905–1961)*

If a man does what is good, let him do it again; let him delight in it; happiness is the outcome of good.
—*Dhammopada*

Noble deeds and hot baths are the best cures for depression. —*Dodie Smith (1896-)*

There are two ways of spreading light: to be the candle or the mirror that reflects it.
—*Edith Wharton (1862–1937)*

Dying legacies are a miserable substitute for living benevolence. —*Ellen G. White (1827–1915)*

Doing good is the easiest way to get the most out of life.— *Elmer G. Leterman (1898-)*

The gentle mind by gentle deeds is known. —*Edmund Spenser (1552–1599)*

One great, strong unselfish soul in every community could actually redeem the world.
—*Elbert Hubbard (1856–1915)*

Our worth is determined by the good deeds we do, rather than by the fine emotions we feel.
—*Elias L. Magoon (1810–1886)*

Idealists . . . foolish enough to throw caution to the winds . . . have advanced mankind and have enriched the world. —*Emma Goldman (1869–1940)*

Good will, like a good name, is got by many actions and lost by one. —*Francis Jeffrey (1773–1850)*

We must do good to others because it's the right thing to do— not to make ourselves look good.
—*Fritz Guy (1930-)*

Every person is responsible for all the good within the scope of his abilities, and for no more, and none can tell whose sphere is the largest. —*Gail Hamilton (1911-)*

Therefore, as we have opportunity, let us do good to all people. —*Galatians 6:10 (NIV)*

Let us not be weary in well doing: for in due season we shall reap, if we faint not. —*Galatians 6:9*

I always seek the good that is in people and leave the bad to Him who made mankind and knows how to round off the corners. —*Goethe's Mother*

There is something in benevolent purpose, as well as in industry, that cheers and supports the mind.
—*Hannah Franham Lee (1780–1865)*

But do not forget to do good and to share, for with such sacrifices God is well pleased. —*Hebrews 13:16*

Goodness is the only investment that never fails. —*Henry David Thoreau (1817–1862)*

There cannot be a more glorious object in creation than a human being replete with benevolence, meditating in what manner he may render himself most acceptable to the Creator by doing good to his creatures. —*Henry Fielding (1707–1754)*

It is good to think well; it is divine to act well. —*Horace Mann (1796–1859)*

Beneficence is a duty; and he who frequently practices it and sees his benevolent intentions realized, at length comes to love him to whom he has done good. — *Immanuel Kant (1724–1804)*

Learn to do good, to be fair and to help the poor, the fatherless, and widows. — *Isaiah 1:17 (LB)*

Look for strength in people, not weakness; for good, not evil. Most of us find what we search for.
—J. Wilbur Chapman (1859–1918)

One day you've got to realize that resources don't belong to you. . . . Work with God to plant seeds in the lives of other people. —Jack Eckerd (1913-)

The essence of true nobility is neglect of self. —James A. Froude (1818–1894)

If the word integration means anything, this is what it means: that we, with love, shall force our brothers to see themselves as they are, to cease fleeing from reality and begin to change it.
—James Baldwin (1924–1987)

Never have we performed an act more God-like than when we bring sunshine to hearts that are dark and desolate. —James Gibbons (1834–1921)

There is an aura of victory that surrounds a person of goodwill. —James L. Fisher (1931-)

All of our institutions must now turn their full attention to the great task ahead—to humanize our lives and thus to humanize our society. —James Perkins (1847–1910)

Every man feels instinctively that all the beautiful sentiments in the world weigh less than a single lovely action. —James Russell Lowell (1819–1891)

Only by giving, only by serving, only by doing, do we really do something for ourselves.
—James W. Frick (1924-)

Private beneficence is totally inadequate to deal with the vast numbers of the city's disinherited.
—Jane Adams (1860–1935)

The accumulation of small, optimistic acts produces quality in our culture and in your life. Our culture resonates in tense times to individual acts of grace. —Jennifer James (1943-)

My hope still is to leave this world a little better for my being here. —Jim Henson (1936–1990)

If our entire society is to be revitalized, it will depend on what we as individual Americans are willing to do on our own, in association with others, and how willing we are to extend ourselves beyond our own personal interests. —John D. Rockefeller, III (1906–1978)

I believe that every right implies a responsibility; every opportunity, an obligation; every possession, a duty.
—John D. Rockefeller, Jr. (1874–1960)

I count all that part of my life lost which I spent not in communion with God, or in doing good.
—*John Donne (1573–1631)*

To do something, however small, to make others happier and better, is the highest ambition, the most elevating hope, which can inspire a human being. —*John Lubbock (1834–1913)*

Good, the more communicated, more abundant grows. —*John Milton (1608–1674)*

The way we treat another human being is the way we treat our Lord. That doesn't need further explanation as much as it needs contemplation. —*John P. Hallin (1946-)*

Societies are renewed . . . by people who believe in something, care about something, stand for something.
—*John W. Gardner (1912-)*

All the beautiful sentiments in the world weigh less than one lovely action.
—*James Russell Lowell (1819–1891)*

Do all the good you can,
By all the means you can,
In all the ways you can,
In all the places you can,
At all the times you can,
To all the people you can,
As long as you ever can.
—*John Wesley (1703–1791)*

Shall we call ourselves benevolent, when the gifts we bestow do not cost us a single privation?
—*Joseph Degerando (1772–1844)*

Perdition shall be the lot of man, except for those who have faith and do good works and exhort each other to justice and fortitude. —*Koran, Sura CIII.2,3*

To the good I would be good; to the not-good I would also be good, in order to make them good.
—*Lao-tzu (604–531 B.C.)*

The simplest and shortest ethical precept is to be served as little as possible . . . and to serve others as much as possible. —*Leo Tolstoy (1828–1910)*

We do not love people so much for the good they have done us, as for the good we have done them.
—*Leo Tolstoy (1828–1910)*

Today we are afraid of simple words like goodness and mercy and kindness. We don't believe in the good old words because we don't believe in the good old values anymore.— *Lin Yutang (1895–1976)*

The greatest comfort of my old age, and that which gives me the highest satisfaction, is the pleasing remembrance of the many benefits and friendly offices I have done to others.
—*Marcus Cato (234–149 B.C.)*

In nothing do men approach so nearly to the gods as doing good to their fellowman.
— *Marcus Tullius Cicero (106–43 B.C.)*

Children must have at least one person who believes in them. It could be a counselor, a teacher, a preacher, a friend. It could be you. You never know when a little love and support will plant a small seed of hope. —*Marian Wright Edelman (1940-)*

Always do right. This will gratify some people, and astonish the rest. —*Mark Twain (1835–1910)*

Goodwill is the one and only asset that competition cannot undersell or destroy.
—*Marshall Field (1835–1906)*

The greatest good a man can do is to cultivate himself in order that he may be of greater use to humanity.
—*Marshall Field (1835–1906)*

The time is always right to do what is right. —*Martin Luther King, Jr. (1929–1968)*

When you look for the good in others, you discover the best in yourself. —*Martin Walsh (1938-)*

The age looks steadily to the redressing of wrong, to the righting of every form of error and injustice, and a tireless . . . philanthropy, which . . . is one of the most hopeful characteristics of our time.
—*Mary Livermore (1820–1905)*

Let your light so shine before men that they may see your good works, and glorify your Father which is in heaven. —*Matthew 5:16*

Benevolence is the distinguishing characteristic of man. As embodied in man's conduct, it is called the path of duty. —*Mencius (372–289 B.C.)*

What does the Lord require of you but to do justice, and love kindness, and to walk humbly with your God?
—*Micah 6:8*

Good actions ennoble us, and we are the sons of our own deeds. —*Miguel de Cervantes (1547–1616)*

The good Lord has been good to me, and I am trying to return the favor. I just want to do as much good in the world as I can. —*Milton Petrie (1902-)*

Nothing is more powerful than an individual acting out of his conscience, thus helping to bring the collective conscience to life. —*Norman Cousins (1912-)*

Learn the luxury of doing good. —*Oliver Goldsmith (1728–1774)*

I have . . . a desire to leave the world a little more human than if I had not lived; for a true humanity is . . . our nearest approach to Divinity. —*Oliver Wendell Holmes (1809–1894)*

A different world cannot be built by indifferent people. —*Peter Marshall (1902–1949)*

Think about things that are pure and lovely, and dwell on the fine, good things in others.
—*Philippians 4:8 (LB)*

No man or woman of the humblest sort can really be strong, gentle, pure, and good without the world being better for it, without somebody being helped and comforted by the very existence of that goodness.
—*Phillips Brooks (1835–1893)*

If thine enemy be hungry, give him bread to eat; and if he be thirsty give him water to drink.
—*Proverbs 25:21*

Turn from evil and do good; seek peace and pursue it. —*Psalms 34:14 (NIV)*

Every little deed counts . . . . Every word has power and we can, everyone, do our share to redeem the world.
—*Rabbi Abraham Joshua Heschel (1907–1972)*

Each time a man stands up for an ideal, or acts to improve the lot of others, or strikes out against injustice, he sends forth a tiny ripple of hope. —*Robert F. Kennedy (1925–1968)*

Don't judge each day by the harvest you reap but by the seeds you plant.
—*Robert Louis Stevenson (1850–1894)*

The good that is in you is the good that you do for others. —*Roger Babson (1875–1967)*

To have beauty is to have only that, but to have goodness is to be beautiful too. —*Sappho (c.6 B.C.)*

Fear less, hope more; eat less, chew more; whine less, breathe more; talk less, say more; hate less, love more; and all good things are yours. —*Swedish Proverb*

Benevolence is a natural instinct of the human mind; when A sees B in distress, his conscience always urges him to entreat C to help him. —*Sydney Smith (1771–1845)*

Hold fast that which is good. —*I Thessalonians 5:21*

It is the glory of the true religion that it inculcates and inspires a spirit of benevolence. It is a religion of charity, which none other ever was. —*Thomas Fuller (1654–1734)*

This country will not be a good place for any of us to live in unless we make it a good place for all of us to live in. —*Theodore Roosevelt (1858–1919)*

The smallest actual good is better than the most magnificent promises of impossibilities. —*Thomas B. Macaulay (1800–1859)*

Politeness has been well defined as benevolence in small things. —*Thomas B. Macaulay (1800–1859)*

I believe that every human mind feels pleasure in doing good to another. —*Thomas Jefferson (1743–1826)*

The world is my country, all mankind are my brethren, and to do good is my religion. —*Thomas Paine (1737–1809)*

Benevolence is the characteristic of the righteous descendants of the seed of Abraham, our father. —*Torah*

Some people are benevolent; others are beneficent. The first are well-wishing; the second are well-doing. —*Unknown*

Magnanimous people have no vanity, they have no jealousy, they have no reserves, and they feed on the true and solid wherever they find it. And what is more, they find it everywhere. —*Van Wyck Brooks (1886–1963)*

The only way to compel men to speak good of us is to do it. —*Voltaire (1694–1778)*

The mark of an immature man is that he wants to die nobly for a cause, while the mark of a mature man is that he wants to live humbly for one. —*Wilhelm Stekel (1868–1940)*

He that does good for good's sake seeks neither praise nor reward, but is sure of both in the end. —*William Penn (1644–1718)*

Benevolence doesn't consist in those who are prosperous pitying and helping those who are not. Benevolence consists in fellow-feeling that puts you upon actually the same level with the fellow who suffers. —*Woodrow Wilson (1856–1924)*

Do good and ask not for whom. —*Yiddish Proverb*

Execute true judgment, and shew mercy and compassion every man to his brother. —*Zechariah 7:9*

He who lengthens the life of a poor man has his own life lengthened when his time to die arrives. —*Zohar*

Doing good to others is not a duty. It is a joy, for it increases your own health and happiness. —*Zoroastrian Scriptures*

CHARITY

**Generosity • Grace • Benevolence
Mercy • Compassion**

I have a simple philosophy. Fill what's empty. Empty what's full. And scratch where it itches.
— *Alice Roosevelt Longworth (1884–1980)*

The influence of a beautiful, helpful character is contagious, and may revolutionize a whole town.
—*Eleanor H. Porter (1868–1920)*

I shall do more whenever I shall believe doing more will help the cause.
—*Abraham Lincoln (1809–1865)*

With malice toward none; with charity for all; with firmness in the right, as God gives us to see the right, let us strive on to finish the work we are in. —*Abraham Lincoln (1809–1865)*

The suffering of little children is not what is so intolerable, but the fact that it is undeserved.
—*Albert Camus (1913–1960)*

It is every man's obligation to put back into the world at least the equivalent of what he takes out of it.
—*Albert Einstein (1879–1955)*

Man can find meaning in life only through devoting himself to society. —*Albert Einstein (1879–1955)*

What we do for ourselves dies with us—what we do for others remains and is immortal.
—*Albert Pike (1809–1891)*

In faith and hope the world will disagree, but all mankind's concern is charity.
—*Alexander Pope (1688–1744)*

The size of a person's world is the size of his heart. —*Alfred A. Monatpert (1906-)*

Don't tell me that you're pitiful because you're homeless. You just need some help; ain't nothing pitiful about that. —*Alice Harris Watts—aka Sweet Alice (1937-)*

Never cease to be convinced that life might be better—your own and others'.
—*Andre Gide (1869–1951)*

Don't be content with doing only your duty. Do more than your duty. It's the horse who finishes a neck ahead who wins the race. —*Andrew Carnegie (1835–1919)*

In bestowing charity, the main consideration should be to help those who will help themselves; to provide part of the means by which those who desire to improve may do so; . . . to assist, but rarely or never to do all.
—*Andrew Carnegie (1835–1919)*

He who has never denied himself for the sake of giving, has but glanced at the joys of charity.
—*Anne Swetchine (1782–1857)*

To be a man is to feel that one's own stone contributes to building the edifice of the world.
—*Antoine de Saint Exupery (1900–1944)*

We can do noble acts without ruling earth and sea. —*Aristotle (384–322 B.C.)*

The big problem is not the haves and the have-nots — it's the give-nots. —*Arnold Glasow*

The act of philanthropy is a spiritual act, an expression of caring for one's fellow human beings. It is a belief in the future that the future can be good. It is investing in that future. It is helping to make the dream come true.— *Arthur C. Frantzreb (1920-)*

The word philanthropy has its roots in the Greek language meaning "love for mankind." It was never meant to apply only to donors of thousands or millions of dollars. — *Arthur C. Frantzreb (1920-)*

Believe in something larger than yourself. . . . Get involved in some of the big ideas of your time.
—*Barbara Bush (1925-)*

To gain that which is worth having, it may be necessary to lose everything else.
—*Bernadette Devlin* (1947-)

I don't think you can do anything for anyone without giving up something of your own.
—*Bernard Malamud (1914–1986)*

After the verb "to love," "to help" is the most beautiful verb in the world.
—*Bertha von Suttner (1848–1914)*

We are not cisterns made for hoarding; we are channels made for sharing. —*Billy Graham (1918-)*

If you haven't got any charity in your heart, you have the worst kind of heart trouble.
—*Bob Hope (1903-)*

There's something wonderfully rewarding in being part of an effort that does make a difference. And there's something sparkling about being among other people when they're at their best, too.
— *Brian O'Connell (1930-)*

Through our voluntary organizations and the giving that supports them, ever more Americans worship freely, study quietly, are cared for compassionately, experiment creatively, advocate aggressively and contribute generously. These national traits are constantly beautiful and must remain beautifully constant.
—*Brian O'Connell (1930-)*

In the community sense, caring and service are giving and volunteering. —*Brian O'Connell (1930-)*

Though I speak with the tongues of men and of angels, and have not charity, I am become as sounding brass or a tinkling cymbal. —*I Corinthians 13:1*

And now abideth faith, hope, charity, these three; but the greatest of these is charity.
—*I Corinthians 13:13*

No person was ever honored for what he received. Honor has been the reward for what he gave.
—*Calvin Coolidge (1872–1933)*

Charity is "lending to the Lord, who in good time will return the gift with increase."
—*Calvinist reformers*

Giving a few dollars to a blind beggar or a destitute orphan may be characterized as charity; a large gift of money to an educational institution or a symphony orchestra is philanthropy. —*Carl Bakal (1918-)*

There is a subtle, semantic distinction between charity and philanthropy, although the latter carries with it more of the connotation of large-scale giving—and not necessarily to the poor and suffering.
—*Carl Bakal (1918-)*

The dead hold in their hands only what they have given away. —*Carl Sandburg (1878–1967)*

Charity, the mother of patience, has given her as a sister to obedience, and so closely united them together that one can not be lost without the other. Either thou hast both or thou hast neither.
—*Catherine of Siena (1347–1380)*

Through charity to God we conceive virtues, and through charity toward our neighbors, they are brought to the birth. —*Catherine of Siena (1347–1380)*

Did universal charity prevail, earth would be heaven, and hell a fable.
—*Charles Caleb Colton (1780–1832)*

No one is useless in this world who lightens the burdens of another. —*Charles Dickens (1812–1870)*

Good will is the mightiest practical force in the universe. —*Charles Fletcher Dole (1845–1927)*

Feel for others—in your pocket. —*Charles H. Spurgeon (1834–1892)*

I would like to die a poor man. —*Chester F. Carlson (1906–1968)*

A bit of fragrance always clings to the hand that gives you roses. —*Chinese Proverb*

An institution or reform movement that is not selfish, must originate in the recognition of some evil that is adding to the sum of human suffering. . . . It is a philanthropic movement to try to reverse the process.
—*Clara Barton (1821–1921)*

If you want to do something to help change your world, you can do that—one child at a time.
—*Clifton Davis (1945-)*

It is better to light one small candle than to curse the darkness. —*Confucius (551–479 B.C.)*

There are so many hungry people that God cannot appear to them except in the form of bread.
—*Corita Kent (1918-)*

You have not done enough, you have never done enough, so long as it is still possible that you have something to contribute. —*Dag Hammarskjold (1905–1961)*

What a man does for others, not what they do for him, gives him immortality.
—*Daniel Webster (1782–1852)*

Two phrases—"Will you help?" and "Yes, I will!"—comprise the most beautiful duet in American history. *—David S. Ketchum (1920-)*

There is no better time than right now to start your own "family tradition" of helping needy children. *—Debby Boone (1956-)*

What's important? That I'm fair and honest, and that perhaps along life's way, I can help others. *—Deborah Norville (1958-)*

Children are very precious. We are blessed to have them, but we are blessed even more if we take care of them and see to their needs. *—Delores Bennett (1934-)*

Thou shalt open thine hand wide unto thy brother, to thy poor, and to thy needy, in the land. *—Deuteronomy 15:11*

We are our brothers' keepers and we must not only care for his needs as far as we are immediately able, but we must try to build a better world. *—Dorothy Day (1897–1980)*

The poor man needs not a program, not a plan, just food and a home. *—Dorothy Day (1897–1980)*

The two most beautiful words in the English language are: 'Check enclosed.' *—Dorothy Parker (1893–1967)*

Charitable planning is the process of doing better by doing good. *—Douglas K. Freeman (1945-)*

If you want to know the value of an individual, ask not for the sum of all that he owns, but look instead to the total of all that he has given. *—Douglas K. Freeman (1945-)*

Cast thy bread upon the waters: for thou shalt find it after many days. *—Ecclesiastes 11:1*

The blessings we evoke for another descend upon ourselves. *—Edmund Gibson (1892–1962)*

All that we send into the lives of others, comes back into our own. *—Edwin Markham (1852–1940)*

Down in their hearts, wise men know this truth: the only way to help yourself is to help others. *—Elbert Hubbard (1856–1915)*

What shall I do with my life? How much am I willing to give of myself, of my time, of my love? *—Eleanor Roosevelt (1884–1962)*

When you cease to make a contribution you begin to die. *—Eleanor Roosevelt (1884–1962)*

The spirit of Christian liberality will strengthen as it is exercised. —*Ellen G. White (1827–1915)*

The spirit of liberality is the spirit of heaven. —*Ellen G. White (1827–1915)*

The law of self-sacrifice is the law of self-preservation.—*Ellen G. White (1827–1915)*

No other influence that can surround the human soul has such power as the influence of an unselfish life. —*Ellen G. White (1827–1915)*

I have never been especially impressed by the heroics of people convinced that they are about to change the world. I am more awed by. . . those who . . . struggle to make one small difference after another. —*Ellen Goodman (1941-)*

A man has made at least a start on discovering the meaning of human life when he plants shade trees under which he knows full well he will never sit. —*Elton Trueblood (1900-)*

Charity is to will and do what is just and right in every transaction. —*Emanuel Swedenborg (1688–1772)*

True charity is the desire to be useful to others without thought of recompense. —*Emanuel Swedenborg (1688–1772)*

Great thoughts speak only to the thoughtful mind, but great actions speak to all mankind. — *Emily P. Bissell (1861–1948)*

Give me your tired, your poor, your huddled masses yearning to breathe free, the wretched refuse of your teeming shore. Send these, the homeless, the tempest-tossed to me, I lift my lamp beside the golden door. —*Emma Lazarus (1849–1887)*

Live and work to make a difference, to make things better, even the smallest things. Give full consideration to the rights and interests of others. No business is successful, even if it flourishes, in a society that does not care for or about its people. —*Eugene C. Dorsey (1927-)*

Charity separates the rich from the poor; aid raises the needy and sets him on the same level with the rich. —*Eva Peron (1919–1952)*

How in the world could I have lived such a helpful life as I have lived had I not been blind? —*Fanny Crosby (1820–1905)*

In charity there is no excess. —*Francis Bacon (1561–1626)*

The Golden Rule is of no use to you whatever unless you realize that it is your move.
—*Frank Crane (1861–1928)*

Your sole contribution to the sum of things is yourself. —*Frank Crane (1861–1928)*

Charity literally means love, the love that understands, that does not merely share the wealth of the giver, but in true sympathy and wisdom helps men to help themselves. —*Franklin D. Roosevelt (1882–1945)*

The future must be seen in terms of what a person can do to contribute something, to make something better, to make it go where he believes with all his being it ought to go. —*Frederick R. Kappel (1902-)*

Sacrifice alone, bare and unrelieved, is ghastly, unnatural, and dead; but self-sacrifice, illuminated by love, is warmth, and life. —*Frederick William Robertson (1816–1853)*

Helpfulness to others is the best kind of good. —*Fritz Guy (1930-)*

The command to give charity weighs as much as all the other commandments put together. . . . He who gives alms in secret is greater than Moses. —*Gemara - Baba Bathra*

Poverty is more grievous than fifty plagues. —*Gemara - Baba Bathra*

We are not the sum of our possessions. . . . Let us be a thousand points of light to help people.
—*George Bush (1924-)*

Too often we hand folks over to God's mercy, and show none ourselves. —*George Eliot (1819–1880)*

I believe that every sacrifice we make will so enrich us in the future that our regret will be that we did not enrich the sacrifice the more. . . . —*George F. Burba (1865–1920)*

To devote a portion of one's leisure to doing something for someone else is one of the highest forms of recreation.— *Gerald B. Fitzgerald (1906-)*

If a man had only his personal interest to guide his conduct, even if this guide were never to deceive him . . . the source of all generous actions would dry up in his heart. —*Germaine de Stael (1766–1817)*

Charity sees the need; not the cause. —*German Proverb*

Give me the ready hand rather than the ready tongue. —*Giuseppe Garibaldi (1807–1882)*

The government has a very critical role to play in a very large range of social problems . . . but social problems will be solved only after every organization pitches in to help. —*Gregg Petersmeyer (1949-)*

The most charitable person is he who gladly effaces himself that he may bestow his favors anonymously.
—*Harry Moyle Tippett (1891–1974)*

I believe that people will do what is right and good if they are given a chance and are convinced that what they are being asked to do will truly help others. —*Helen Boosalis (1919-)*

We are trying to help those with whom we are dealing to find a new meaning in their lives by caring for causes of significance beyond their own self interest. —*Helen Boosalis (1919-)*

Although the world is full of suffering, it is also full of the overcoming of it. —*Helen Keller (1880–1968)*

Not until we can refuse to take without giving, can we create a society in which the chief activity is the common welfare. —*Helen Keller (1880–1968)*

Sure the world is full of trouble, but as long as we have people undoing trouble we have a pretty good world. —*Helen Keller (1880–1968)*

People who give are rewarded, not monetarily, but because their involvement represents an expression beyond themselves. —*Henry A. Rosso (1917-)*

A rich man without charity is a rogue; and perhaps it would be no difficult matter to prove that he is also a fool. —*Henry Fielding (1707–1754)*

Riches without charity are worth nothing. They are a blessing only to him who makes them a blessing to others. —*Henry Fielding (1707–1754)*

When lack of funds prevents hospitals from functioning efficiently and fully, private philanthropy of all kinds must help. The difference it makes . . . in terms of human betterment, represents the kind of happiness that money really can buy. —*Henry T. Heald (1904–1975)*

The poor too often turn away, unheard, from hearts that shut against them with a snap that will be heard in heaven. —*Henry Wadsworth Longfellow (1807–1882)*

Every charitable act is a stepping stone towards heaven. —*Henry Ward Beecher (1813–1887)*

We have not yet reached the goal but . . . we shall soon, with the help of God, be in sight of the day when poverty shall be banished from this nation. —*Herbert C. Hoover (1874–1964)*

To pity distress is but human; to relieve it is godlike. —*Horace Mann (1796–1859)*

The impersonal hand of government can never replace the helping hand of a neighbor.
—*Hubert H. Humphrey (1911–1978)*

We will be remembered not for the power of our weapons but for the power of our compassion, our dedication to human welfare. —*Hubert H. Humphrey (1911–1978)*

If anyone has material possessions and sees his brother in need but has no pity on him, how can the love of God be in him? —*I John 3:17 (NIV)*

God likes help when helping people. —*Irish Proverb*

A bone to the dog is not charity. Charity is the bone shared with the dog when you are just as hungry as the dog. —*Jack London (1876–1916)*

The boundaries of altruism are not even limited to an infinite sum of currency.
—*Jackie A. Strange (1927-)*

Every man has a mission from God to help his fellow beings. —*James Gibbons (1834–1921)*

A candle loses nothing of its light by lighting another candle. —*James Keller (1900–1977)*

Do not wait for extraordinary circumstances to do good actions; try to use ordinary circumstances.
—*Jean Paul Richter (1763–1825)*

The last, best fruit which comes to late perfection, even in the kindliest soul, is tenderness toward the hard, forbearance toward the unforbearing, warmth toward the cold, philanthropy toward the misanthropic.
—*Jean Paul Richter (1763–1825)*

What you give for the cause of charity in health is gold; what you give in sickness is silver; what you give after death is lead.— *Jewish Proverb*

Charity is the spice of riches.— *Jewish Proverb*

The only true charity is so contrived that the recipient need beg no more.
— *Johann Pestalozzi (1746–1827)*

Knowing is not enough; we must apply. Willing is not enough; we must do.
—*Johann Wolfgang von Goethe (1749–1832)*

We can offer up much in the large, but to make sacrifices in little things is what we are seldom equal to.
—*Johann Wolfgang von Goethe (1749–1832)*

We would give more alms if we had the eyes to see what a beautiful picture a receiving hand makes.
—*Johann Wolfgang von Goethe (1749–1832)*

He who bestows his goods upon the poor,
Shall have as much again, and ten times more.
— *John Bunyan (1628–1688)*

This only is charity, to do all, all that we can. —*John Donne (1573–1631)*

Our responsibility is not discharged by the announcement of virtuous ends.
—*John F. Kennedy (1917–1963)*

If we who have, cannot help those who have not, then we cannot help ourselves.
—*John F. Kennedy (1917–1963)*

The critics were asking that we postpone consideration of the causes of poverty until no one was poor.
— *John Kenneth Galbraith (1908-)*

How difficult it is to be wisely charitable—to do good without multiplying the source of evil. To give alms
is nothing unless you give thought also. —*John Ruskin (1819–1900)*

By doing good with his money, a man, as it were, stamps the image of God upon it, and makes it pass
current for the merchandise of heaven. —*John Rutledge (1739–1800)*

For every talent that poverty has stimulated it has blighted a hundred. —*John W. Gardner (1912-)*

Charity is a virtue of the heart. Gifts and alms are the expressions, not the essence, of this virtue.
—*Joseph Addison (1672–1719)*

Charity is the perfection and ornament of religion. —*Joseph Addison (1672–1719)*

Be charitable and indulgent to everyone but thyself. —*Joseph Joubert (1754–1824)*

Pity costs nothin, and ain't worth nothin'. —*Josh Billings (1818–1885)*

It is well to give when asked, but it is better to give unasked, through understanding.
—*Kahlil Gibran (1883–1931)*

Whatever ye put out at usury to increase it with the substance of others shall have no increase from God;
but whatever ye shall give in alms, as seeking the face of God, shall be doubled to you. —*Koran*

Prayer carries us half-way to God, fasting brings us to the door of his palace, and alms giving procures us
admission. —*Koran*

Woe to those who pray but are heedless in their prayer; who make a show of piety and give no alms to the destitute. —*Koran, Sura CVII.4-7*

Be neither miserly nor prodigal, for then you should either be reproached or be reduced to penury. —*Koran, Sura XVII.31*

I truly enjoy no more of the world's good things than what I willingly distribute to the needy. —*Lucius Annaeus Seneca (4 B.C.–A.D.65)*

He that does good to another, does good also to himself, not only in the consequences, but in the very act; for the consciousness of well-doing is, in itself, ample reward. —*Lucius Annaeus Seneca (4 B.C.–A.D.65)*

As ye would that men should do to you, do ye also to them. —*Luke 6:31*

I am convinced that we must train not only the head, but the heart and hand as well. —*Madame Chiang Kai-Shek (1898-)*

When profit is unshared it's less likely to grow greater. —*Malcolm S. Forbes (1919–1990)*

You can easily judge the character of others by how they treat those who can do nothing for them or to them. —*Malcolm S. Forbes (1919–1990)*

Your purse should not be closed so tightly that a kind impulse is not able to open it. —*Marcus Tullius Cicero (106–43 B.C.)*

Necessity can set me helpless on my back, but she cannot keep me there; nor can four walls limit my vision. —*Margaret Fairless Barber (1869–1901)*

To insure the continuity of philanthropy, we must instill in kids the values and attitudes that will enable them to see charity as a vital part of their lives. —*Mary Leonard (1952-)*

Philanthropy is one of the most hopeful characteristics of our time. —*Mary Livermore (1820–1905)*

We know God wipes away all tears, but it certainly feels good when He uses human hands. —*Mary Paulson-Lauda (1916-)*

Go and sell what thou hast, and give to the poor, and thou shalt have treasures in heaven. —*Matthew 19:21*

Inasmuch as ye have done it unto one of the least of these my brethren, ye have done it unto me. —*Matthew 25:40*

To live is not to live for one's self; let us help one another. —*Menander of Athens (342-291 B.C.)*

I will charge thee nothing but the promise that thee will help the next man thee finds in trouble. —*Mennonite Proverb*

It is not the shilling I give you that counts, but the warmth that it carries with it from my hand. —*Miguel de Unamuno (1864–1936)*

Hope in action is charity, and beauty in action is goodness. —*Miguel de Unamuno (1864–1936)*

To keep a lamp burning, we have to keep putting oil in it.— *Mother Teresa (1910-)*

There is always the danger that we may become only social workers, or just do the work for the sake of the work. It is a danger if we forget to whom we are doing it. —*Mother Teresa (1910-)*

If you really love one another properly, there must be sacrifice. —*Mother Teresa (1910-)*

War on nations changes maps. War on poverty maps change. —*Muhammad Ali (1769–1849)*

It is the nature of men to be as much bound by the benefits that they confer as by those they receive. —*Niccolo Machiavelli (1469–1527)*

The great thing in this world is not so much where we stand, as in what direction we are moving. —*Oliver Wendell Holmes (1809–1894)*

You cannot function with maximum effectiveness on behalf of a cause in which you do not fully believe and to which you yourself have not made a financial contribution. —*Paul H. Schneiter (1935-)*

I know we have a generation out there that doesn't care about anything except making money, but I think the '90s could easily go back to social involvement like the '60s. —*Paul Simon (1942-)*

To do good things in the world, first you must know who you are and what gives meaning in your life. —*Paula P. Brownlee (1934-)*

We need to restore the full meaning of that old word, duty. It is the other side of rights. —*Pearl S. Buck (1892–1973)*

To give to the poor is to share one's self; to give to the rich is to share one's ego. —*Pedrito U. Maynard-Reid (1947-)*

Being sensitive to the needs of the oppressed poor, creates a new world in which all persons affirm their full sense of humanity. —*Pedrito U. Maynard-Reid (1947-)*

Often the best way of giving oneself what one lacks is to take from oneself what one has. —*Persian Proverb*

Focus on the contribution that you can make. —*Peter Drucker (1909-)*

Small deeds done are better than great deeds planned. —*Peter Marshall (1902–1949)*

There is a wonderful mythical law of nature that the three things we crave most in life—happiness, freedom and peace of mind—are always attained by giving them to someone else. —*Peyton Conway March (1864–1955)*

Charity withers in the incessant gale. —*Phyllis McGinley (1905–1978)*

Make us worthy, Lord, to serve our fellow men throughout the world who live and die in poverty and hunger. —*Pope Paul VI (1897–1978)*

The American people have a genius for splendid and unselfish action, and into the hands of America, God has placed the destinies of afflicted humanity. —*Pope Pius XII (1876–1958)*

Charity and pride have different aims, yet both feed the poor. —*Proverb*

If you would have a blessing upon your riches, bestow a good portion of them in charity.— *Proverb*

He who shuts his ear to the cry of the poor will also cry himself and not be answered. —*Proverbs 21:13 (NASV)*

Withhold not good from them to whom it is due, when it is in the power of thine hand to do it. —*Proverbs 3:27*

Honor the Lord with . . . the first fruits of all thine increase. So shall thy barns be filled with plenty. —*Proverbs 3:9-10*

He upholds the cause of the oppressed and gives food to the hungry. —*Psalms 146:7 (NIV)*

Blessed is he that considereth the poor. —*Psalms 41:1*

We are here to change the world with small acts of thoughtfulness done daily rather than with one great breakthrough. —*Rabbi Harold Kushner (1935-)*

Let man realize that he himself is forever seeking sustenance at the hand of God, and just as God answers his prayer, so should he answer the prayer of the poor. —*Rabbi Joseph Karo (1488–1575)*

Everyone is obliged to contribute to charity. —*Rabbi Joseph Karo (1488–1575)*

Anticipate charity by preventing poverty. —*Rabbi Moses ben Maimon "Maimonide" (1135–1204)*

Before prayer, give to charity. —*Rabbi Nahman ben Simha (1770–1811)*

A person's proximity to God is measured by his compassion toward his fellow man.
—*Rabbi Samuel Belkin (1900–1982)*

It is one of the most beautiful compensations of this life that no man can sincerely try to help another without helping himself. —*Ralph Waldo Emerson (1803–1882)*

In necessary things, unity; in doubtful things, liberty; in all things, charity.
—*Richard Baxter (1615–1691)*

There is probably no more moral activity than the self-sacrifice involved in donating one's blood.
— *Richard F. Schubert (1936-)*

People think that if they were rich they would contribute to charities. My experience has been if you don't start giving away your money when you have very little, you won't do it when you get a lot.
— *Robert Bainum (1925-)*

Man's inhumanity to man makes countless thousands mourn! —*Robert Burns (1759–1796)*

I would help others, out of a fellow-feeling. —*Robert Burton (1577–1640)*

The superior man rises by lifting others. —*Robert G. Ingersoll (1833–1899)*

The hands that help are holier than the lips that pray. —*Robert G. Ingersoll (1833–1899)*

We rise by raising others—and he who stoops above the fallen, stands erect.
—*Robert G. Ingersoll (1833–1899)*

There is no doubt that the poorer classes in our country are much more charitably disposed than their superiors in wealth. —*Robert Louis Stevenson (1850–1894)*

By working together, pooling our resources and building on our strengths, we can accomplish great things.
—*Ronald Reagan (1911-)*

We owe it to the unfortunate to be aware of their plight and to help them in every way we can.
—*Ronald Reagan (1911-)*

Through the history of our nation, Americans have always extended their hands in gestures of assistance.
—*Ronald Reagan (1911-)*

To take the neediest class we know—both in poverty and suffering—and put them in such a condition that if our Lord knocked at the door I should not be ashamed to show what I have done. This is a great hope.... —*Rose Hawthorne Lathrop (1851–1926)*

It was on my fifth birthday that Papa put his hand on my shoulder and said, 'Remember, my son, if you ever need a helping hand, you'll find one at the end of your arm.' —*Sam Levenson (1911–1980)*

A decent provision for the poor is the true test of civilization. —*Samuel Johnson (1709–1784)*

Liberality consists less in giving a great deal than in gifts well-timed. —*Samuel Johnson (1709–1784)*

He who waits to do a great deal of good at once, will never do anything.
—*Samuel Johnson (1709–1784)*

Bounty always receives part of its value from the manner in which it is bestowed.
—*Samuel Johnson (1709–1784)*

Charity begins at home, but should not end there. —*Scottish Proverb*

I really want to leave the world better than I found it. —*Sebastian S. Kresge (1867–1966)*

It is all right your saying you do not need other people, but there are a lot of people who need you.
—*Sherwood Anderson (1876–1941)*

Charity: To love human beings ... as God does. —*Simone Weil (1909–1943)*

The most noble charity is to prevent our neighbor from having the need to accept charity, and the best gift is to teach and assist our neighbors in giving freely. —*Sina M. Reid (1942-)*

The race of mankind would perish from the earth did they cease to aid each other.
—*Sir Walter Scott (1771–1832)*

Who does not befriend himself by doing good? —*Sophocles (495–406 B.C.)*

By always taking out and never putting in, the bottom is soon reached. —*Spanish Proverb*

As a torch is not diminished though it kindles a million candles, so will he not lose when he gives to a good cause. —*The Midrash*

Charity is equal to all the other precepts put together. —*The Talmud*

Charity is offered with one's money; kindness, with both one's person and one's money. Charity is bestowed on the poor; kindness upon both poor and rich. —*The Talmud*

Charity knows neither race nor creed. —*The Talmud*

The greatest charity is to enable the poor to earn a living. —*The Talmud*

The noblest charity is to prevent a man from accepting charity; and the best alms are to show and to enable a man to dispense with alms. —*The Talmud*

Whoever would change men must change the conditions of their lives. —*Theodor Herzl (1860–1904)*

To be permanently effective, aid must always take the form of helping a man to help himself. —*Theodore Roosevelt (1858–1919)*

Do what you can, with what you have, where you are. —*Theodore Roosevelt (1858–1919)*

No man is worth his salt who is not ready at all times to risk his body, to risk his well-being, to risk his life, in a great cause. —*Theodore Roosevelt (1858–1919)*

Do what lieth in thy power, and God will assist in thy good will. —*Thomas a'Kempis (1380–1471)*

He is truly great who hath a great charity. —*Thomas a'Kempis (1380–1471)*

Charity brings to life again those who are spiritually dead. —*Thomas Aquinas (1225–1274)*

True charity is sagacious, and will find out hints for beneficence. —*Thomas Browne (1605–1682)*

He hath riches sufficient, who hath enough to be charitable. —*Thomas Browne (1605–1682)*

Not what I have but what I do is my kingdom. —*Thomas Carlyle (1795–1881)*

Two things a man should never be angry at: what he can help and what he can't help. —*Thomas Fuller (1654–1734)*

There can be no greater argument to a man of his own power than to find himself able not only to accomplish his own desires, but also to assist other men in theirs; and this is that conception wherein consisteth charity. —*Thomas Hobbes (1588–1679)*

I deem it the duty of every man to devote a certain portion of his income for charitable purposes; and that it is his further duty to see it so applied; to do the most good of which it is capable. — *Thomas Jefferson (1743–1826)*

We have contributed, each in the time allotted us, our endeavors to render . . . a permanent blessing to our country. — *Thomas Jefferson (1743–1826)*

Lay on your children the obligation to behave uprightly, to give alms, to keep God in mind and to bless His name always, sincerely and with all their might. —*Tobit 14:8*

To enable others to look beyond themselves and their immediate concerns, and to give without expectation of fanfare represents the most vital contribution of the quiet hero. —*Unknown*

Give as the sun gives light, a glad outpouring of the best that is in you. —*Unknown*

Charity begins at home, and generally dies from lack of outdoor exercise. —*Unknown*

The basic and fundamental reason for giving has been to fill a need. —*Unknown*

We hold in our hands the power to lift each other up to new heights of humanity or to let go, plunging mankind into an abyss of destruction. —*Unknown*

Charity is no substitute for justice withheld. —*Unknown*

The best kind of charity is the kind that helps others to eliminate any further need of it. —*Unknown*

When it comes to helping you, some people stop at nothing. —*Unknown*

Charity of thought, word, or deed always leads to the most lasting honors man can attain. —*Unknown*

People give from the heart, not from economics. When a need is recognized, the heart moves the hand. —*Unknown*

The charitable give out at the door and God puts in at the window. —*Unknown*

To place your name, by gift or bequest, in the keeping of a healing hospital is to be sure that the name and project with which it is associated will continue through the years to save lives and restore health, thus making a permanent contribution to the welfare of mankind. —*Unknown*

The greatest strength of character is magnanimity. —*Unknown*

Real charity doesn't care if it's tax-deductible or not. —*Unknown*

Most of us will never do great things, but we can do small things in a great way. —*Unknown*

The kind of charity that does you the most good is the giving-in kind. —*Unknown*

Learn to care and share with others; have faith and trust in them and you will find these assets for yourself. —*Unknown*

If you are not poor enough to take charity, you are rich enough to give it. —*Unknown*

There is one pleasure that the human being cannot tire of and that is the pleasure that comes from helping someone who really needs you. —*Unknown*

If you give away your money to charity while you are alive, your relatives won't have to fight over it when you are dead. —*Unknown*

Some people are so nearsighted that they can't see the need for charity until they're up against it. —*Unknown*

Be more charitable: don't follow the path of least assistance. —*Unknown*

One of the best ways to do yourself a favor is to lend somebody else a helping hand. —*Unknown*

How long will it take us to learn that there are only two things in life that really count—one is character and the other is human sympathy. —*Unknown*

What is charity? It is silence—when your words would hurt. It is patience—when your neighbor is hurt. It is deafness—when a scandal flows. It is thoughtfulness—for others' woes. It is promptness—when duty calls. It is courage—when misfortune falls. —*Unknown*

The true value of human life is determined by the extent to which it is used to help others. —*Val Halamandaris (1942-)*

As the purse is emptied the heart is filled. —*Victor Hugo (1802–1885)*

We are all here on earth to help others; what on earth the others are here for I don't know.
—*W. H. Auden (1907–1973)*

Charity and personal force are the only investments worth anything. —*Walt Whitman (1819–1892)*

The race of mankind would perish did they cease to aid each other. We cannot exist without mutual help. All, therefore, that need aid have a right to ask it from their fellow-men; and no one who has the power of granting can refuse it without guilt. —*Walter D. Scott (1869–1955)*

It's nice to know that we don't need to wait till tomorrow, we can start to change the world today!
—*Wil Rose (1931–)*

That's one trouble with our charities: we are always saving somebody away off, when the fellow next to us ain't eating. —*Will Rogers (1879–1935)*

There is no charity in a man's leaving money in his will; he has simply got to leave it. The time to administer your trust is while you are still living. —*William Gladstone (1809–1898)*

That charity which longs to publish itself, ceases to be charity. —*William Hutton (1723–1815)*

Do good with what thou hast, or it will do thee no good. —*William Penn (1644–1718)*

'Tis not enough to help the feeble up, but to support him after. —*William Shakespeare (1564–1616)*

My good will is great, though the gift small. —*William Shakespeare (1564–1616)*

My purse, my person, my extremist means, lie all unlock'd to your occasion.
—*William Shakespeare (1564–1616)*

Sweet mercy is nobility's true badge. —*William Shakespeare (1564–1616)*

People that trust wholly to other's charity, and without industry of their own, will always be poor.
—*William Temple (1881–1944)*

The charities that soothe and heal and bless are scattered at the feet of man like flowers.
—*William Wordsworth (1770–1850)*

Provision for others is a fundamental responsibility of human life. —*Woodrow Wilson (1856–1924)*

You can get everything in life that you want . . . if you'll just help enough other people get what they want.
—*Zig Ziglar (1926–)*

CHRISTMAS
Cheer • Love • Good Will
Giving • Holiday

Christmas is glorious. I love the season, the spirit of Christmas. If your heart is in the right place, it affords you appropriate opportunity to do things for others, to express your good will, to let yourself go sentimentally and philanthropically. —*B. C. Forbes (1880–1954)*

Anything that inspires unselfishness makes for our ennoblement. Christmas does that. I am all for Christmas. —*B. C. Forbes (1880–1954)*

Christmas is not a time or a season but a state of mind. To cherish peace and good will, to be plenteous in mercy, is to have the real spirit of Christmas. — *Calvin Coolidge (1872–1933)*

I will honor Christmas in my heart, and try to keep it all the year. —*Charles Dickens (1812–1870)*

Christmas, my child, is love in action. . . . Every time we love, every time we give, it's Christmas. —*Dale Evans Rogers (1912-)*

I sometimes think we expect too much of Christmas Day. We try to crowd into it the long arrears of kindliness and humanity of the whole year. —*David Grayson (1870–1945)*

May you have the greatest two gifts of all on these holidays: Someone to love and someone who loves you. —*John Sinor (1930-)*

Christmas is not a date. It is a state of mind. —*Mary Ellen Chase (1887–1973)*

Christmas is a holiday that we celebrate not as individuals nor as a nation, but as a human family. —*Ronald Reagan (1911-)*

Giving is just making Christmas out of every day that comes with an opportunity to help. Giving makes a holiday for the soul. —*T. T. Frankenberg (1877–1958)*

The spirit of Christmas is always near; it shines like a beacon throughout the year. Don't look in a store or high on a shelf, for sharing and giving are found in yourself. —*Unknown*

Christmas began in the heart of God. It is complete only when it reaches the heart of man. —*Unknown*

God bless your Christmas Season with happy days of cheer. God keep His richest favors and all His blessings near. God grant you after Christmas a bright and blessed New Year. —*Unknown*

The message of Christmas is that the visible material world is bound to the invisible spiritual world. —*Unknown*

What the New Year will bring us depends a great deal on what we bring to the New Year. —*Unknown*

Christmas is the season for kindling the fire of hospitality in the hall, the genial flame of charity in the heart. —*Washington Irving (1783–1859)*

EDUCATION

**Instruction • Schooling • Teaching • Wisdom
Training • Learning • Knowledge**

Don't ever dare to take your college as a matter of course—because, like freedom and democracy, many people you'll never know anything about have broken their hearts to get it for you.
—*Alice Duer Miller (1874–1942)*

The most beautiful thing in the world is the conjunction of learning and inspiration.
—*Alice Wanda Landowski (1899–1959)*

All human wisdom is summed up in two words—wait and hope. —*Alexandre Dumas (1802–1870)*

Those who would administer wisely must, indeed, be wise, for one of the serious obstacles to the improvement of our race is indiscriminate charity. —*Andrew Carnegie (1835–1919)*

All who have meditated on the art of governing mankind have been convinced that the fate of empires depends on the education of youth. —*Aristotle (384–322 B.C.)*

The good Education of Youth has been esteemed by wise men of all ages, as the surest foundation of the happiness both of private families and of commonwealths. —*Benjamin Franklin (1706–1790)*

To place your name by gift or bequest in the keeping of an active educational institution is to. . .make a permanent contribution to the welfare of humanity. —*Calvin Coolidge (1872–1933)*

Whoever acquires knowledge but does not practice it is like one who ploughs a field but does not sow it.
—*Calvin Coolidge (1872–1933)*

Tell me, I'll forget. Show me, I may remember. But involve me, and I'll understand. —*Chinese Proverb*

It is, sir, as I have said, a small college—and yet there are those who love it.
—*Daniel Webster (1782–1852)*

Let us develop the resources of our land, call forth its powers, build up its institutions, promote all its great interest, and see whether we also, in our day and generation, may not perform something worthy to be remembered. —*Daniel Webster (1782–1852)*

Education is the controlling grace to the young, consolation to the old, wealth to the poor, and ornament to the rich. —*Diogenes Laertius (c. 200)*

The mintage of wisdom is to know that rest is rust and that real life is in love, laughter, and work.
—*Elbert Hubbard (1856–1915)*

Our beliefs as well as our actions must come from the heart, for in our hearts the true wisdom that frees us and the path of compassion are inseparable. —*Bstan'dzin-rgya-mtsho (1935-)*

Opportunity is what America is all about, and education is the key to opportunity. It's a ticket out of poverty. —*George Bush (1924-)*

If we are to improve our standard of living, protect and defend our democratic freedom, and strengthen our moral character as a nation, nothing is more important than education. —*George Bush (1924-)*

Education—a debt due from present to future generations. —*George Peabody (1795–1869)*

Education, in the broadest and truest sense, will make an individual seek to help all people, regardless of race, regardless of color, regardless of condition. —*George Washington Carver (1865–1943)*

A good education is a stepping stone to wealth. —*Helen Keller (1880–1968)*

My darkness has been filled with the light of intelligence, and behold, the outer day lit world was stumbling and groping in social blindness. —*Helen Keller (1880–1968)*

The best-educated human being is the one who understands most about the life in which he is placed.
—*Helen Keller (1880–1968)*

Education is the knowledge of how to use the whole of oneself. —*Henry Ward Beecher (1813–1887)*

The great aim of education is not knowledge but action. —*Herbert Spencer (1820–1903)*

Around every college and university in this nation there exists a handful of people who literally make these institutions go. These are those people who hold the future of the institution in their hands, who make today's dreams, tomorrow's realities. —*James W. Frick (1924-)*

No student ever pays the full cost of his education. We've all been helped by our college to achieve success . . . and we owe it to ourselves to put something back in the pot. —*Janet Harris (1932–1979)*

The man who gives an adequate gift to a well-equipped American college is more sure of an earthly immortality than any other private citizen. —*James A. Michener (1907-)*

One mother achieves more than a hundred teachers. —*Jewish Proverb*

Higher education must lead the march back to the fundamentals of human relationships, to the old discovery that is ever new, that man does not live by bread alone. —*John A. Hannah (1902-)*

Our progress as a nation can be no swifter than our progress in education. . . . The human mind is our fundamental resource. —*John F. Kennedy (1917–1963)*

Let us think of education as the means of developing our greatest abilities, because in each of us there is . . . a dream which, fulfilled, can be translated into benefit for everyone and greater strength for our nation. —*John F. Kennedy (1917–1963)*

Education . . . which makes men happiest in themselves also makes them more serviceable to others. —*John Ruskin (1819–1900)*

If a man empties his purse into his head, no man can take it away from him, for an investment in knowledge pays the best interest. —*Joseph E. O'Donnell, Jr. (1961-)*

That is what our educational system has to encourage. It has to foster the social goals of living together, and working together, for the common good. —*Julius Nyerere (1922-)*

Our education must therefore inoculate a sense of commitment to the total community, and help the pupils to accept the values appropriate to our kind of future. . . . —*Julius Nyerere (1922-)*

The excellence and freedom of a university depend on a sufficient measure of private support and endowment by people who believe in it, and indeed who love it. —*Katherine Meyer Graham (1917-)*

Real education should educate us out of self into something far finer—into a selflessness which links us with all humanity. —*Lady Nancy Astor (1879–1964)*

Iron rusts from disuse, stagnant water loses its purity, and in cold weather water becomes frozen; even so does inaction sap the vigors of the mind. —*Leonardo da Vinci (1452–1519)*

The best of all things is to learn. Money can be lost or stolen, health and strength may fail, but what you have committed to your mind is yours forever. —*Louis L'Amour (1908–1988)*

What greater or better gift can we offer the republic than to teach and instruct our youth.
—*Marcus Tullius Cicero (106–43 B.C.)*

When schools flourish, all flourish. —*Martin Luther (1483–1546)*

Higher education and business are basically interdependent. One needs money to produce educated people, and the other needs educated people to produce money. —*Milton S. Eisenhower (1899–1985)*

God has given us enough wisdom to make improvements in our relations.
—*Mikhail S. Gorbachev (1931-)*

Learn to give money to colleges while you live. Don't be silly and think you'll try to bother colleges when you die. —*Oliver Wendell Holmes (1809–1894)*

If a man be endowed with a generous mind, this is the best kind of nobility. —*Plato (427–347 B.C.)*

He that is void of wisdom despiseth his neighbor: but a man of understanding holdeth his peace.
—*Proverbs 11:12*

When you give to aid scholars, you gain a share in their learning.
— *Rabbi Nahman ben Simha (1770–1811)*

Few expenditures we can make yield a greater return than those for education. A well-educated person produces more and consumes more, makes wiser decisions at the pools, mounts a stronger defense against aggression, and is better able to perform the grave responsibilities of American citizenship.
—*Ralph J. Cordiner (1900-)*

No college or university . . . is so generously supported by tuition, government grants, or income from endowments that it can ignore the need to systematically and vigorously develop the additional resources it must have from private gifts. —*Robert L. Payton (1926-)*

Philanthropy is an important subject of liberal education because it examines the role of good works in shaping our conceptions of the good society and the good life. —*Robert L. Payton (1926-)*

Alumni support is a financial way of showing love—the greatest motivation for giving.
—*Roger Craver (1941-)*

We must join together—parents, teachers, grass-roots groups, organized labor and the business community—to revitalize American education by setting a standard of excellence.
—*Ronald Reagan (1911-)*

The University, like other great institutions of higher education in this country, must have adequate endowment to remain secure against the unreliability of public policy.
—*The John Hopkins University Case Statement*

If the condition of man is to be progressively ameliorated . . . . Education is to be the chief instrument in effecting it. —*Thomas Jefferson (1743–1826)*

And now that you're a distinguished alumnus, you'll be interested to know that the college has launched a fund-raising drive! —*Unknown*

The students ask why, the faculty asks how, and the alumni asks how much. —*Unknown*

A school is a building that has four walls and a tomorrow inside. —*Unknown*

Money is never so honored as when it is being used to educate the young. —*Unknown*

Alumnafied: a neologism of recent coinage; to become identified once more with the needs of one's educational institution. —*Unknown*

Education is not the filling of a pail, but the lighting of a fire. —*William Butler Yeats (1865–1939)*

Books are the true levelers. They give to all, who faithfully use them, the society, the spiritual presence, and the best and greatest of our race. —*William Ellery Channing (1780–1842)*

It is no longer our resources that limit our decisions; it's our decisions that limit our resources.
—*U. Thant (1909–1974)*

❦

FRIENDSHIP

Brotherhood • Comradeship • Intimacy
Relationships • Neighborly

Little friends may prove great friends. —*Aesop (620–560 B.C.)*

Only those who respect the personality of others can be of real use to them.
—*Albert Schweitzer (1875–1965)*

The salvation of mankind lies only in making everything the concern of all.
—*Alexander Solzhenitsyen (1918-)*

Friendship consists in forgetting what one gives and remembering what one receives.
—*Alexandre Dumas the Younger (1824–1895)*

Each friend represents a world in us, a world possibly not born until they arrive, and it is only by this meeting that a new world is born. —*Anais Nin (1903–1977)*

We forget that there is no hope of joy except in human relations.
—*Antoine de Saint-Exupery (1900–1944)*

A faithful friend is a strong defense: and he that hath found such one hath found a treasure. —*Apocrypha*

A faithful friend is the medicine of life. —*Apocrypha*

A sweet word multiplieth friends, and appeaseth enemies, and a gracious tongue in a good man aboundeth. —*Apocrypha*

Nothing can be compared to a faithful friend, and no weight of gold and silver is able to countervail the goodness of his fidelity. —*Apocrypha*

A friend is one to whom we may pour out the contents of our hearts, chaff and grain together, knowing that the gentlest of hands will sift it, keep what is worth keeping, and with a breath of kindness blow the rest away. —*Arabian Definition*

A true friend is one soul in two bodies. —*Aristotle (384–322 B.C.)*

Without friends no one would choose to live, though he had all other goods. —*Aristotle (384–322 B.C.)*

At the end of your life, you will never regret not having passed one more test, not winning one more verdict or not closing one more deal. You will regret time not spent with a husband, a friend, a child or a parent. —*Barbara Bush (1925-)*

Wherever our life touches yours we help or hinder. There is no escape—man drags man down, or man lifts man up. —*Booker T. Washington (1856–1915)*

Brotherhood is the very price and condition of man's survival. —*Carlos P. Romulo (1901-)*

True friendship is like sound health, the value of it is seldom known until it is lost. —*Charles Caleb Colton (1780–1832)*

If we would build on a sure foundation in friendship, we must love our friends for their sakes rather than for our own. —*Charlotte Bronte (1816–1855)*

We won't always know whose lives we touched and made better for our having cared, because actions can sometimes have unforeseen ramifications. What's important is that you do care and you act. —*Charlotte Lunsford (1931-)*

It takes a year to make a friend, but you can lose one in an hour. —*Chinese Proverb*

What brings joy to the heart is not so much the friend's gift as the friend's love. —*Eden Phillpotts (1862–1960)*

If a friend is in trouble, don't annoy him by asking if there is anything you can do. Think up something appropriate and do it. —*Edgar Watson Howe (1853–1937)*

Too many of us stay walled up because we are afraid of being hurt. We are afraid to care too much, for fear that the other person does not care at all. —*Eleanor Roosevelt (1884–1962)*

The most important thing in any relationship is not what you get but what you give . . . . In any case the giving of love is an education in itself. —*Eleanor Roosevelt (1884–1962)*

A friend in need is a friend indeed. —*English Proverb*

It is a good thing to be rich and a good thing to be strong, but it is a better thing to be beloved of many friends. —*Euripides (480–406 B.C.)*

If a man be gracious and courteous to strangers, it shows he is a citizen of the world, and that his heart is no island, cut off from other lands, but a continent that joins to them. —*Francis Bacon (1561–1626)*

Love is blind; friendship closes its eyes. —*French Proverb*

Until you have become a brother to everyone, brotherhood will not come to pass.
—*Feodor Dostoevski (1821–1881)*

Be a loyal friend, a loving parent, a citizen who leaves home, neighborhood, and town better for having lived for others. —*George Bush (1924-)*

What do we live for if it is not to make life less difficult for each other? —*George Eliot (1819–1880)*

It is not by driving away our brother that we can be alone with God. —*George MacDonald (1824–1905)*

Actions, not words, are the true criterion of the attachment of friends; and the most liberal professions of good-will are very far from being the surest marks of it. —*George Washington (1732–1799)*

True friendship is a plant of slow growth and must undergo and withstand the shocks of adversity before it is entitled to the appellation. —*George Washington (1732–1799)*

The man who thinks he can live without others is mistaken; the one who thinks others can't live without him is even more deluded. —*Hasidic Proverb*

We must not only affirm the brotherhood of man; we must live it.
—*Henry Codman Potter (1835–1908)*

Make a better friend of every man with whom you come in contact. —*Henry L. Doherty (1870–1939)*

In the New Year, may your right hand always be stretched out in friendship, but never in want.
— *Irish Toast*

The opportunity to practice brotherhood presents itself every time you meet a human being.
—*Jane Wyman (1914-)*

Treat your friends as you do your pictures, and place them in their best light.
—*Jennie Jerome Churchill (1854–1921)*

Friendship . . . is the golden thread that ties the heart of all the world. —*John Evelyn (1620–1706)*

Friendship is always a sweet responsibility, never an opportunity. —*Kahlil Gibran (1883–1931)*

Good and evil deeds are not alike. Requite evil with good, and he who is your enemy will become your dearest friend. —*Koran, Sura XLI.34*

There is nothing more important in life than human beings, nothing sweeter than the human touch.
—*Lee Atwater (1951–1991)*

We are each of us angels with only one wing. And we can only fly embracing each other.
—*Luciano de Crescenzo (1928-)*

We were born to unite with our fellowmen, and to join in community with the human race.
—*Marcus Tullius Cicero (106–43 B.C.)*

Friendship renders prosperity more brilliant, while it lightens adversity by sharing it and making its burden common. —*Marcus Tullius Cicero (106–43 B.C.)*

Now that's a real diamond—the person that will take time to be a friend to those in need and not just the people with pleasing personalities. —*Maxine Blome (1928-)*

Silence makes the real conversations between friends. Not the saying, but the never needing to say is what counts. —*Margaret Lee Runbeck (1910–1956)*

The true neighbor will risk his position, his prestige, and even his life for the welfare of others.
—*Martin Luther King, Jr. (1929–1968)*

In dangerous valleys and hazardous pathways, the true neighbor will lift some bruised and beaten brother to a higher and more noble life. —*Martin Luther King, Jr. (1929–1968)*

The poor are our brothers and sisters. . . . They are the people in the world who need love, who need care, who have to be wanted. —*Mother Teresa (1910-)*

There is a magnet in your heart that will attract true friends. That magnet is unselfishness, thinking of others first. . . . When you learn to live for others, they will live for you.
—*Paramahansa Yogananda (1893–1952)*

He who helps a child helps humanity with an immediateness which no other help given . . . in any other stage of human life can possibly give again. —*Phillips Brooks (1835–1893)*

What is thine is mine, and all mine is thine. —*Plautus (250–184 B.C.)*

Your wealth is where your friends are. —*Plautus (250–184 B.C.)*

Make not thy friend too cheap to thee, nor thyself to thy friend. —*Proverb*

A friend loveth at all times. . . . —*Proverbs 17:17*

A man that hath friends must show himself friendly: and there is a friend that sticketh closer than a brother. —*Proverbs 18:24*

You don't have to act as if you care; you just have to care enough to act. —*Richard Dreyfuss (1947-)*

So long as we love, we serve. So long as we are loved by others, I would almost say we are indispensable; and no man is useless while he has a friend. —*Robert Louis Stevenson (1850–1894)*

A friend is a gift you give yourself. —*Robert Louis Stevenson (1850–1894)*

No distance of place or lapse of time can lessen the friendship of those who are thoroughly persuaded of each other's worth. —*Robert Southey (1744–1843)*

In believing in others, we are believed. In supporting others, we gain followers, and in recognizing the value of others, we are honored. —*Solon B. Cousins (1925-)*

Adversity not only draws people together but brings forth that beautiful inward friendship, just as the cold winter forms ice-figures on the window-panes which the warmth of the sun effaces. —*Soren Kierkegaard (1813–1855)*

None of us has gotten where we are solely by pulling ourselves up from our own bootstraps. We got here because somebody. . . bent down and helped us. —*Thurgood Marshall (1908–1993)*

Fundamental sincerity is the only proper basis for forming a relationship. —*Unknown*

God cares for people through people. —*Unknown*

Living is the art of loving,
Loving is the art of caring,
Caring is the art of sharing,
Sharing is the art of living.
—*Unknown*

Friends tie their purse with a cobweb thread. —*Unknown*

What is as important as knowledge? Caring, and seeing with the heart. —*Unknown*

Empathy feels these thoughts; your hurt is in my heart, your loss is in my prayers, your sorrow is in my soul, and your tears are in my eyes. —*William Arthur Ward (1921-)*

Friendship, like money, is a trust, a stewardship, a responsibility. —*William Arthur Ward (1921-)*

I am wealthy in my friends. —*William Shakespeare (1564–1616)*

One touch of nature makes the whole world kin. —*William Shakespeare (1564–1616)*

Only free peoples can hold their purpose and their honor steady to a common end and prefer the interest of mankind to any narrow interest of their own. —*Woodrow Wilson (1856–1924)*

Friendship is the only cement that will ever hold the world together. —*Woodrow Wilson (1856–1924)*

GENEROSITY
**Liberal • Unselfish • Magnanimous
Freehanded • Unsparing**

Too many have dispensed with generosity to practice charity. —*Albert Camus (1913–1960)*

Real generosity toward the future consists in giving all of what is present. —*Albert Camus (1913–1960)*

Generosity is not merely a trait that pleases God; it is a practice which releases us from bondage to the ego, and also to things. —*Albert E. Day (1884–1973)*

When I find a great deal of gratitude in a poor man, I take it for granted there would be as much generosity if he were rich. —*Alexander Pope (1688–1744)*

Many men have been capable of doing a wise thing, more a cunning thing, but very few a generous thing. —*Alexander Pope (1688–1744)*

A man is sometimes more generous when he has but a little money than when he has plenty, perhaps through fear of being thought to have but little. —*Benjamin Franklin (1706–1790)*

In five ways should a clansman minister to his friends and familiars—by generosity, courtesy, and benevolence, by treating them as he treats himself, and by being as good as his word. —*Buddha (556–480 B.C.)*

You will be made rich in every way so that you can be generous on every occasion, and through us your generosity will result in thanksgiving to God. —*II Corinthians 9:11*

One of the finest virtues is generosity—a quality characteristic of the person who thinks more highly of others than he does of himself. —*D. Malcolm Maxwell (1934-)*

Generosity is good deeds that are done quietly, inconspicuously and are immediately forgotten.
—*Dave Grant (1939-)*

Acts of generosity and benevolence were designed by God to keep the hearts of the children of men tender and sympathetic, and to encourage in them an interest and affection for one another, in imitation of the Master, who for our sakes became poor, that we through his poverty might be made rich.
—*Ellen G. White (1827–1915)*

Never measure your generosity by what you give, but rather by what you have left.
—*Fulton J. Sheen (1895–1979)*

Kindness and generosity . . . form the true morality of human actions.
—*Germaine de Stael (1766–1817)*

Generosity is something we learn, from our parents, schools and community. —*H. Ross Perot (1930-)*

America has a long and rich tradition of generosity that began with simple acts of neighbor helping neighbor. —*Helen Boosalis (1919-)*

The truly generous is the truly wise, and he who loves not others, lives unblest.
—*Henry Home (1696–1782)*

When you give, take to yourself no credit for generosity, unless you deny yourself something in order that you may give. —*Henry Taylor (1800–1886)*

He who gives what he would as readily throw away, gives without generosity; for the essence of generosity is in self-sacrifice. —*Henry Taylor (1800–1886)*

Watch lest prosperity destroy generosity. —*Henry Ward Beecher (1813–1887)*

Generosity during life is a very different thing from generosity in the hour of death; one proceeds from genuine liberality and benevolence, the other from pride and fear. —*Horace Mann (1796–1859)*

The poor don't know that their function in life is to exercise our generosity.
—*Jean-Paul Sartre (1905–1980)*

It's hard to outdo the Lord in generosity. —*Jerold Panas (1928-)*

There is not another country in the world that can come close to matching the generosity of Americans. And each year we give more. —*Jerold Panas (1928-)*

Generosity is giving more than you can; pride is taking less than you need.
—*Kahlil Gibran (1883–1931)*

Generosity is not in giving me that which I need more than you do, but it is in giving me that which you need more than I do. —*Kahlil Gibran (1883–1931)*

Money-giving is a good criterion of a person's mental health. Generous people are rarely mentally ill people. —*Karl Menninger (1893–1990)*

It is not in everyone's power to secure wealth, office, or honors; but everyone may be good, generous, and wise. —*Luc de Clapiers Vauvenargues (1715–1747)*

Generosity should never exceed ability. —*Marcus Tullius Cicero (106 –43 B.C.)*

We simply cannot delegate the exercise of mercy and generosity to others. —*Margaret Thatcher (1925-)*

Generosity is a principle—not an amount. —*Millie Thornton (1958-)*

Suffering can become a means to greater love and greater generosity. —*Mother Teresa (1910-)*

True generosity does not consist in obeying every impulse of humanity. . . so as to render us incapable of future ones. —*Oliver Goldsmith (1728–1774)*

True generosity is a duty as indispensably necessary as those imposed on us by law.
—*Oliver Goldsmith (1728–1774)*

A really great man is known by three signs: Generosity in the design, humanity in the execution, moderation in success. —*Otto Eduard Leopold von Bismarck (1815–1898)*

Good will comes to him who is generous and lends freely, who conducts his affairs with justice.
—*Psalms 112:5*

Be generous, and you will be prosperous. Help others, and you will be helped. —*Proverbs 11:25 (GNB)*

Be generous and share your food with the poor. You will be blessed for it. —*Proverbs 22:9 (LB)*

When it comes to generosity, the spirit of service to our fellow human beings regardless of nationality or race or creed, I risk incurring the sin of pride by saying no nation exceeds our own.
—*Richard F. Schubert* (1936-)

There is not a more useful man in the commonwealth than a good physician; and by consequence no worthier a person than he that uses his skill with generosity, and compassion. —*Richard Steele (1917-)*

The record of a generous life runs like a vine around the memory of our dead, and every sweet unselfish act is now a perfumed flower. —*Robert G. Ingersoll (1833–1899)*

There never was any heart truly great and generous, that was not also tender and compassionate. —*Robert South (1634–1716)*

To be wealthy, a rich nature is the first requisite and money but the second. To be of a quick and healthy blood, to share in all honorable curiosities, to be rich in admiration and free from envy, to rejoice greatly in the good of others, to love with such generosity of heart that your love is still a dear possession in absence or unkindness—these are the gifts of fortune which money cannot buy, and without which money can buy nothing. —*Robert Louis Stevenson (1850–1894)*

I am confident that the character and generosity of our people will never erode. —*Ronald Reagan (1911-)*

He who allows his day to pass by without practicing generosity and enjoying life's pleasures is like a blacksmith's bellows—he breathes but does not live. —*Sanscrit Proverb*

Each of you who has been the recipient of somebody's generosity should try to remember that in your life, and preferably while you are living, do something about that. —*Terry Bennett (1938-)*

Thoughtfulness for others, generosity, modesty and self-respect are the qualities which make a real gentleman or lady. —*Thomas Huxley (1825–1895)*

The test of generosity is not how much you give, but how much you have left. —*Unknown*

Some people think they are generous because they give away free advice. —*Unknown*

Never suppress a generous impulse. —*Unknown*

How delightful is the company of generous people, who overlook trifles and keep their minds instinctively fixed on whatever is good and positive in the world about them. —*Van Wyck Brooks (1886–1963)*

Be generous! Give to those you love; give to those who love you; give to the fortunate; give to the unfortunate—yes, give especially to those to whom you don't want to give. You will receive abundance for your giving. The more you give, the more you will have! —*W. Clement Stone (1902-)*

I can remember way back when a liberal was one who was generous with his own money. —*Will Rogers (1879–1935)*

A generous action is its own reward. —*William Walsh (1663–1708)*

Real and lasting generosity requires that a person do more than make up his mind to give. He must also make up his heart. —*William Arthur Ward (1921-)*

Service is love made visible. Generosity is caring made active. Friendship is trust made manifest. —*William Arthur Ward (1921-)*

Generous deeds would be repeated oftener if more gratitude had been shown for the first ones. —*William Feather (1870–1944)*

GIVING

**Bestow • Provide • Gift • Charity
Donate • Present**

It is more blessed to give than to receive. —*Acts* 20:35

The value of a man should be in what he gives and not in what he is able to receive.
—*Albert Einstein (1879–1955)*

You must give some time to your fellow man. Even if it's a little thing, do something for those who have need of help, something for which you get no pay but the privilege of doing it. For remember, you don't live in a world all your own. Your brothers are here, too. —*Albert Schweitzer (1875–1965)*

It is more difficult to give money away intelligently than it is to earn it in the first place.
—*Andrew Carnegie (1835–1919)*

Do your givin' while you're livin'. . . then you'll be knowin' where it's goin'. —*Ann Landers (1918-)*

To give without any reward, or any notice, has a special quality of its own. It is like presents made for older people when you were a child. —*Anne Morrow Lindbergh (1906-)*

Do right to the widows, judge for the fatherless, give to the poor, defend the orphan, clothe the naked.
—*Apocrypha*

A liberal man is one who gives the right thing at the right time to the right person.
—*Aristotle (384–322 B.C.)*

Man holds in his hands through life and hereafter only that which he has given away.
— *Arthur C. Frantzreb (1920-)*

Give with great pride and gratitude for benefits received from our society—never apathy, apology, or embarrassment. Give with a sense of unselfish love for others. —*Arthur C. Frantzreb (1920-)*

A hand not extended in giving is in no position to receive. —*Arthur C. Frantzreb (1920-)*

Each gift contains within its sharing a special magic of its own. —*Arthur C. Frantzreb (1920-)*

All who are served by the health care institution that receives your thoughtful gift will be blessed in perpetuity because you cared and you shared. —*Arthur C. Frantzreb (1920-)*

We insure our valuables; let us insure our values with generous gifts of caring.
—*Arthur C. Frantzreb (1920-)*

Thoughtful giving begins with thoughts on giving. —*Arthur C. Frantzreb (1920-)*

Some people give time, some money, some their skills and connections. Some literally give their life's blood. But everyone has something to give. —*Barbara Bush (1925-)*

Giving frees us from the familiar territory of our own needs by opening our mind to the unexplored worlds occupied by the needs of others. —*Barbara Hand Herrera (1943-)*

To give can be a form of taking; and a donor who distributes money on the basis that he knows what will be best for other people is often resented even more than an impulsive spendthrift.
—*Ben Whitaker (1934-)*

He gives twice that gives soon; i.e., he will soon be called to give again.
—*Benjamin Franklin (1706–1790)*

God has given us two hands—one to receive with and the other to give with. —*Billy Graham (1918-)*

The life worth living is giving for the good of others. —*Booker T. Washington (1856–1915)*

If you are eager to give, God will accept your gift on the basis of what you have to give, not on what you don't have. —*II Corinthians 8:12*

The important thing is to be willing to give as much as we can— that is what God accepts, and no one is asked to give what he has not got. —*II Corinthians 8:12 (Phillips)*

But just as you excel in everything—in faith, in speech, in knowledge, in complete earnestness and in your love for us—see that you also excel in this grace of giving. —*II Corinthians 8:7*

Each man should give what he has decided in his heart to give, not reluctantly or under compulsion, for God loves a cheerful giver. —*II Corinthians 9:7 (NIV)*

The excellence of a gift lies in its appropriateness rather than in its value.
—*Charles Dudley Warner (1829–1900)*

Give because you love to give—as the flower pours forth its perfume.
—*Charles H. Spurgeon (1834–1892)*

Giving is true loving. —*Charles H. Spurgeon (1834–1892)*

It is doubtful if any gift could be brought more precious than the adoration of a heart which has put out all hatred, self-pity and desire for revenge. — *Charlotte Bronte (1816–1855)*

To keep my health!
To do my work!
To live!
To see to it that I grow and gain and give!
—*Charlotte Perkins Gilman (1860–1935)*

Continually give, continually gain. —*Chinese Proverb*

Examples are few of men ruined by giving. Men are heroes in spending, cravens in what they give.
—*Christian Nestell Bovee (1820–1904)*

Give a gift to all generations by saving the earth. —*Christina R. Newman (1946)*

There lies within most of us an innate quality that compels us to give of ourselves for the good of mankind.
—*Clyde G. Kissinger (1926-1978)*

He who gives to me teaches me to give. —*Danish Proverb*

The joy of giving is as often overlooked as the giving of joy. —*David Barton (1924-)*

The habit of giving one's self and one's wealth to other people and higher causes is an acquired characteristic. —*David S. Ketchum (1920-)*

I am firmly determined . . . to give more than I receive. —*Debbye Turner (1965-)*

We must not only give what we have; we must also give what we are.
—*Desiree Joseph Mercier (1851–1926)*

Give generously to him and do so without a grudging heart; then because of this the Lord God will bless you in all your work and in everything you put your hand to. —*Deuteronomy 15:10 (NIV)*

Every man shall give as he is able, according to the blessing of the Lord. —*Deuteronomy 16:17*

Give your gift of love to the community of birth defects. —*Donna F. Garlinghouse (1935-)*

The love of God compels us to give. —*Dorothy Day (1897–1980)*

The will and not the gift makes the giver. —*Doris Lessing (1919-)*

Only those who have nothing in them have nothing to give. —*Douglas G. Franklin (1950-)*

Give of the three things you have: time, talent, treasure. —*Douglas M. Lawson (1936-)*

To live joyfully, one must give spontaneously and freely. —*Douglas M. Lawson (1936-)*

Giving freely is the key to living fully. —*Douglas M. Lawson (1936-)*

When we give of what we have, we are ready to receive what we really need.
—*Douglas M. Lawson (1936-)*

Giving is the investment in living that pays the dividends we need: health and happiness.
—*Douglas M. Lawson (1936-)*

Giving is the secret elixir that gives life meaning. —*Douglas M. Lawson (1936-)*

Giving is the secret to living fully while you are still alive. —*Douglas M. Lawson (1936-)*

Walk in the shoes of a giver and you will find the pathway to joyful living.
—*Douglas M. Lawson (1936-)*

We exist temporarily through what we take, but we live forever through what we give.
—*Douglas M. Lawson (1936-)*

We receive from life what we give to it, and what we give to life we never lose.
—*Douglas M. Lawson (1936-)*

Takers ultimately lose, but givers win forever. This is a rule the universe never breaks.
—*Douglas M. Lawson (1936-)*

We hear a great deal about the Lord loving cheerful givers; we wonder where he finds them.
—*Edgar Watson Howe (1853–1937)*

God let it be known that it is better to give than to receive, but a lot of people failed to get the message.
—*Edmund W. Littlefield (1914-)*

The Lord loveth a cheerful giver, and I can't stand any other kind.
—*Edwin Clarence Norton (1856–1943)*

Blessed are those who can give without remembering and take without forgetting.
—*Elizabeth Bibesco (1897–1945)*

The heart of God yearns over His earthly children with a love stronger than death. In giving up His Son, He has poured out to us all heaven in one gift. —*Ellen G. White (1827–1915)*

Every ray of light that we shed upon others is reflected upon ourselves . . . and every gift to the needy, if prompted by a right motive, will result in blessing to the giver. —*Ellen G. White (1827–1915)*

Our sons and daughters must be trained in national service, taught to give as well as to receive.
—*Emmeline Pankhurst (1858–1928)*

What I gave, I have, what I spent, I had, what I left, I lost by not giving it.
—*Epitaph of Christopher Chapman*

Giving is the highest expression of potency. —*Erich Fromm (1900–1980)*

Not he who has much is rich, but he who gives much. —*Erich Fromm (1900–1980)*

Giving is a habit of the heart. It is not a tax deduction. —*Ernie Wood (1934-)*

It is only in the giving of oneself to others that we truly live. —*Ethel Percy Andrus (1884–1967)*

Those who give five percent of their incomes or volunteer five hours per week should be our models. Like tithers, these fivers represent the ideal of active citizenship and personal community service.
—*Eugene C. Dorsey (1927-)*

Give, if it means to suffer; give, if it means to lose; give, in life; give, in death; give forever throughout eternity. —*Evangeline Booth (1865–1950)*

It is not how many years we live, but what we do with them. It is not what we receive, but what we give to others. —*Evangeline Booth (1865–1950)*

Pity all you like, but for God's sake give! —*Evangeline Booth (1865–1950)*

Speak unto the children of Israel, that they bring me an offering: of every man that giveth it willingly with his heart ye shall take my offering. —*Exodus 25:2*

Take ye from among you an offering unto the Lord: whosoever is of a willing heart, let him bring it, an offering of the Lord; gold, and silver, and brass. —*Exodus 35:5*

The deep rewards of giving go to those who give out of a concern for others, and take pains to see that their giving is wisely done, to meet real needs or seize promising opportunities.
—*F. Emerson Andrews (1902–1978)*

True giving knows no season. —*Florence E. King (1888–1983)*

Nature has made you for a giver: Your hands are born open, and so is your heart.
—*Frances Hodgson Burnett (1849–1924)*

Give whatever you give with pride. Gratitude for your support is not measured by the size of the gift but truly by its significance as measured by you. —*Francis C. Pray (1909–1982)*

The best thing to give to your enemy is forgiveness; to an opponent, tolerance; to a friend, your heart; to your child, a good example; to a father, deference; to your mother, conduct that will make her proud of you; to yourself, respect; to all men, charity. —*Francis Maitland Balfour (1851–1882)*

We give to others not out of a sense of obligation, but out of a sense of sincere appreciation for what our community has given us. —*Frank M. Hubbard (1920-)*

If you haven't experienced the joy of giving, you must learn to. It is a fascinating, ethereal feeling that doesn't come as a result of planning or effort but as a by-product of helping others.
—*Frank M. Hubbard (1920-)*

In all giving, give thought. With thoughtful giving, even small sums may accomplish great purposes.
—*Fred G. Meyer (1886–1978)*

He gives nothing who does not give himself. —*French Proverb*

Should not the giver be thankful that the receiver received? Is not giving a need? Is not receiving, mercy?
—*Friedrich W. Nietzsche (1844–1900)*

Donors don't give to institutions. They invest in ideas and people in whom they believe.
—*G. T. Smith (1935-)*

When you stop giving and offering something to the rest of the world, it's time to turn out the lights.
—*George Burns (1896-)*

Give—and somewhere, from out of the clouds, or from the sacred depths of human hearts, a melody divine will reach your ears, and gladden all your days upon the earth. —*George F. Burba (1865–1920)*

Those who give most, have most left. —*George F. Burba (1865–1920)*

What you are is God's gift to you and what you do with what you are is your gift to God. —*George Foster (1858–1918)*

What we give, forever is our own. —*George Granville (1667–1735)*

A little given seasonably excuses a great gift. —*George Herbert (1593–1633)*

Let thy alms go before, and keep heaven's gate
Open for thee, or both may come too late.
—*George Herbert (1593–1633)*

In giving, a man receives more than he gives, and the more is in proportion to the worth of the thing given. —*George MacDonald (1824–1905)*

Many look with one eye at what they give, but with seven at what they receive. —*German Proverb*

A major gift represents a major commitment on the part of the contributor. That commitment shows up in future gifts and bequests that may be more significant than the capital gift.
—*Harold D. Wilkins (1929-)*

Unless we give part of ourselves away, unless we can live with other people and understand them and help them, we are missing the most essential part of our own human lives. —*Harold Taylor (1914-)*

The most enthusiastic givers in life are the real lovers of life. They experience the soul-joy that comes from responding with the heart rather than the head. —*Helen Steiner Rice (1900–1981)*

Giving is a privilege that fills the heart with joy. —*Henry A. Rosso (1917-)*

The richest gifts we can bestow are the least marketable. —*Henry David Thoreau (1817–1862)*

If you give money, spend yourself with it. —*Henry David Thoreau (1817–1862)*

It is easy to give alms; it is better to work to make the giving of alms unnecessary.
—*Henry Ford (1863–1947)*

The man who will use his skill and constructive imagination to see how much he can give for a dollar, instead of how little he can give for a dollar, is bound to succeed. —*Henry Ford (1863–1947)*

Give what you have. To someone, it may be better than you dare to think.
—*Henry Wadsworth Longfellow (1807–1882)*

In this world, it is not what we take up but what we give up that makes us rich.
—*Henry Ward Beecher (1813–1887)*

To give quickly is a great virtue. —*Hindu Proverb*

Sometimes give your services for nothing, calling to mind a previous benefaction or present satisfaction. And if there be an opportunity of serving one who is a stranger in financial straits, give full assistance to all such. —*Hippocrates (460–377 B.C.)*

Know from the bounteous heavens all riches flow;
and what man gives, the gods by man bestow.
—*Homer (fl. 850 B.C.)*

All that is not given is lost. —*Indian Proverb*

Give cheerfully with one hand and you will gather well with two. —*Irish Proverb*

Share your food with the hungry and open your homes to the homeless . . . Give clothes to those who have nothing to wear and do not refuse to help. —*Isaiah 58:7 (TEV)*

He serves best who gives most of himself. Self is forgotten by the one who serves, for such a one rejoices to see success coming to others through his efforts. —*James Cash Penney (1875–1971)*

How can we expect our children to know and experience the joy of giving unless we teach them that the greater pleasure in life lies in the art of giving rather than receiving. —*James Cash Penney (1875–1971)*

Giving is true living. —*Jack Herman (1923-)*

Every good gift and every perfect gift is from above, and cometh down from the Father of lights.
—*James 1:17*

Not what we give, but what we share, for the gift without the giver is bare.
—*James Russell Lowell (1819–1891)*

You must be fit to give before you can be fit to receive. —*James Stephens (1882–1950)*

I have never seen a person sacrifice to make a contribution. People contribute only that portion of their income which will not in any way infringe upon their standard of living. —*James W. Frick (1924-)*

Giving pays the highest interest rate and has the longest term of any investment available. —*Jeffrey K. Wilson (1944-)*

Give your time to great causes. Let your candle burn at both ends if necessary. It will provide a dazzling light, a beacon for others to follow. —*Jerold Panas (1928-)*

Life is a wheel. The more you give, the more you get back. —*Jerold Panas (1928-)*

Who will not give some portion of his ease, his blood, his wealth . . . f or others' good, is a poor, frozen churl. —*Joanna Baillie (1762–1851)*

For God so loved the world, that He gave His only begotten Son, that whosoever believeth in Him should not perish, but have everlasting life. —*John 3:16*

A man can receive nothing except it be given him from heaven. —*John 3:27*

You have not lived today until you have done something for someone who can never repay you. —*John Bunyan (1628–1688)*

There was a man, though some did count him mad,
the more he cast away the more he had
—*John Bunyan (1628–1688)*

Long ago I lost the joy in living. The only joy I have is in my giving. —*John D. Rockefeller (1839–1937)*

I was trained from the beginning to work, to save, and to give. —*John D. Rockefeller, Jr. (1874–1960)*

Think of giving not as a duty but as a privilege. —*John D. Rockefeller, Jr. (1874–1960)*

Let him give on till he can give no more. —*John Dryden (1631–1700)*

For of those to whom much is given, much is required. —*John F. Kennedy (1917–1963)*

Nothing lifts your spirits or fills your heart more than giving your support and time to a good cause. —*John J. Schwartz (1919-)*

Make all you can, save all you can, give all you can. —*John Wesley (1703–1791)*

All you have shall some day be given; therefore, give now that the season of giving may be yours and not your inheritor's. —*Kahlil Gibran (1883–1931)*

You give but little when you give of your possessions. It is when you give of yourself that you truly give. —*Kahlil Gibran (1883–1931)*

For some, giving is only a painful and necessary act forced by societal and social pressures. But not for good givers—for them, it's a joy. —*Kenneth N. Dayton (1922-)*

Sometimes we don't give generously because we don't see the generous Giver to whom it all belongs anyway! —*Kent R. Hunter (1947-)*

Giving allows me to touch the lives of people I don't even know, but whose lives I would like to help improve. —*L. Stanley Chauvin, Jr. (1935-)*

Giving presents is a talent; to know what a person wants, to know when and how to get it, to give it lovingly, and well. —*Lady Pamela Wyndham Glenconner (1871–1928)*

The American people, over a period of more than two centuries, have already proved that they are willing to contribute generously of their money and goods to help others. —*Landrum R. Bolling (1913-)*

He who obtains has little. He who scatters has much. —*Lao-tzu (604–531 B.C.)*

If you would take, you must first give, this is the beginning of intelligence. —*Lao-tzu (604–531 B.C.)*

Our greatest joy and satisfaction comes from the act of giving. —*Leo Buscaglia (1925-)*

The miracle is this. . . the more we share, the more we have. —*Leonard Nimoy (1931-)*

What you get is a living—what you give is a life. —*Lillian Gish (1893–1993)*

It is another's fault if he be ungrateful; but it is mine if I do not give. —*Lucius Annaeus Seneca (4 B.C.–A.D. 65)*

He who gives when he is asked has waited too long. —*Lucius Annaeus Seneca (4 B.C.–A.D. 65)*

Much is required from those to whom much is given, for their responsibility is greater. —*Luke 12:48 (LB)*

Whatever measure you use to give—large or small—will be used to measure what is given back to you.
—*Luke 6:38 (LB)*

Give to the world the best that you have and the best will come back to you.
—*Madeline Bridges (1844–1920)*

Give thy mind more to what thou hast than to what thou hast not.
—*Marcus Aurelius Antoninus (121–180)*

Give often when you know your gifts are well placed. —*Marcus Cato (234–149 B.C.)*

Give and forgive. —*Marie Therese Rodet Geoffrin (1669–1757)*

Profit is what we have left after we make a donation to a worthwhile cause.
—*Marilyn Vos Savant (1946-)*

What you give away is the only wealth you will always have. —*Martial (40–103)*

The heart of the giver makes the gift dear and precious. —*Martin Luther (1483–1546)*

Giving does not impoverish us in the service of our Maker, neither does withholding enrich us.
—*Mary Baker Eddy (1821–1910)*

God, let me be a giver, and not one
Who only takes and takes unceasingly;
God, let me give, so that not just my own,
But others' lives as well, may richer be.
—*Mary Carolyn Davies (fl. 1920)*

Freely ye have received, freely give. —*Matthew 10:8*

Give to him that asketh thee, and from him that would borrow of thee turn not thou away.
—*Matthew 5:42*

Take heed that ye do not your alms before men, to be seen of them. —*Matthew 6:1*

When thou doest alms, let not thy left hand know what thy right hand doeth; that thine alms may be in secret. —*Matthew 6:3*

To give and then not feel one has given is the very best of all ways of giving.
—*Max Beerbohm (1872–1956)*

We are to give in sincerity, not to make a show of our good deeds. Sincerity of purpose, real kindness of heart, is the motive that heaven values. —*Maxine Blome (1928-)*

Being very rich, as far as I am concerned, is having a margin. The margin is being able to give. —*May Sarton (1912-)*

He that gives quickly gives twice. —*Miguel de Cervantes (1547–1616)*

The more I make, the more I can give away. The good Lord has been good to me, and I'm trying to return the favor. —*Milton Petrie (1902-)*

Youth expects fun in the getting, age reflects on the fun of having given. —*Milton Murray (1922-)*

His alms are vain who does not know that his need of the reward for giving is greater than the poor man's need of the gift. —*Mohammed (570–632)*

Let us not be satisfied with just giving money. Money is not enough; money can be got; but they need your hearts to love them. —*Mother Teresa (1910-)*

Once you pledge, don't hedge. —*Nikita S. Khrushchev (1894–1971)*

Help is giving part of yourself to somebody who comes to accept it willingly and needs it badly. —*Norman Maclean (1902-)*

The secret of the law of abundance is this: In order to receive and appreciate the good things of life, you must first give. —*Norman Vincent Peale (1898–1993)*

Such a simple thing as the giving of yourself—giving thoughtfulness, time, help or understanding—will trigger the cycle of abundance. —*Norman Vincent Peale (1898–1993)*

People fail to understand that unless they are themselves willing to give, they will never receive. —*Norman Vincent Peale (1898–1993)*

If you think you have given enough, think again. There is always more to give and someone to give it to. —*Norman Vincent Peale (1898–1993)*

I give that you may give. —*Otto Eduard Leopold von Bismarck (1815–1898)*

Giving calls for genius. —*Ovid (43 B.C.–A.D. 17)*

He who gives while he lives also knows where it goes. —*Percy Ross (1916-)*

Give plenty of what is given to you, and listen to pity's call; don't think the little you give is great and the much you get is small. —*Phoebe Cary (1824–1874)*

The manner of giving is worth more than the gift. —*Pierre Corneille (1606–1684)*

I would have a man generous to his country, his neighbors, his friends, and most of all his poor friends. Not like some who are most lavish with those who are able to give most to them. — *Pliny the Younger (61–113)*

Gifts break through stone walls. —*Proverb*

Alms-giving never made any man poor, nor robbery rich, nor prosperity wise. —*Proverb*

He that gives to be seen will relieve none in the dark. —*Proverb*

He that giveth unto the poor shall not lack. —*Proverbs 28:27*

A gift is as a precious stone in the eyes of him that hath it. —*Proverbs 17:8*

A man's gift maketh room for him, and bringeth him before great men. —*Proverbs 18:16*

Every man is a friend to him that giveth gifts. —*Proverbs 19:6*

The size of the gift to an institution is not important. No gift is important, no matter how large, unless it means something to the one who gives it. —*R. Blair Schreyer (1925–1985)*

I hate the giving of the hand unless the whole man accompanies it.
—*Ralph Waldo Emerson (1803–1882)*

Rings and jewels are not gifts, but apologies for gifts. The only true gift is a portion of thyself.
—*Ralph Waldo Emerson (1803–1882)*

The giving of blood is imbued with the psychology of peace, for it leaves its humanitarian mark in the hearts of those who give for their fellowman. —*Red Cross Courier (1947)*

It is possible to give without loving, but it is impossible to love without giving.
—*Richard Braunstein (1930-)*

Giving of ourselves is the way we change the world at the end of our fingertips.
—*Richard F. Schubert (1936-)*

The question is not "What can I get?" but "What can I give in life?"
—*Robert Baden-Powell (1858–1941)*

I give because I want to, not because I ought to. I feel good knowing that my gifts of time and money are making a difference in the community and, hopefully, shaping spiritual moral values.
—*Robert Bainum (1925-)*

Give to others so that they may grow strong and not dependent. —*Robert Dole (1923-)*

Giving and receiving are mutual. Receiving without giving causes dependence. Giving without receiving leads to arrogance. —*Robert E. Fogal (1944-)*

Giving never moves in a straight line—it always moves in circles! It goes round . . . and round . . . and round. —*Robert H. Schuller (1926-)*

Give, if thou canst, an alms; if not, afford, instead of that, a sweet and gentle word.
—*Robert Herrick (1591–1674)*

For too many giving is occasional, spasmodic, ill-proportioned. It depends on what is left over when other things have had their full share. Sometimes what it means is that only the small change lying in their pockets goes to the support of good and worthy causes. —*Robert J. McCracken (1904–1973)*

Private voluntary giving will not increase unless there is better and firmer understanding of its importance to our society and the people in it. —*Robert L. Payton (1926-)*

I am in the habit of looking not so much to the nature of a gift as to the spirit in which it is offered.
—*Robert Louis Stevenson (1850–1894)*

If there be a truer measure of a man than by what he does, it must be by what he gives.
—*Robert South (1634–1716)*

Let . . . the alms giver give freely, . . . and those who do works of mercy do them cheerfully. Do not let your love be a pretense. —*Romans 12:8 (JB)*

He that spared not his own Son, but delivered him up for us all, how shall he not with him also freely give us all things? —*Romans 8:32*

If everyone gives one thread, the poor man will have a shirt. —*Russian Proverb*

Let him that desires to see others happy, make haste to give while his gift can be enjoyed, and remember that every moment of delay takes away something from the value of his benefaction.
—*Samuel Johnson (1709–1784)*

We receive but what we give. —*Samuel Taylor Coleridge (1772–1834*

In giving is the true enlightenment. —*Santideva*

He that bringeth a present, findeth the door open. —*Scottish Proverb*

If it is more blessed to give than to receive, then most of us are content to let the other fellow have the greater blessing. —*Shailer Matthews (1863–1943)*

It is better to give than to lend, and it costs about the same. —*Sir Philip Gibbs*

For it is by giving that one receives, it is by self-forgetting that one finds, it is by forgiving that one is forgiven. —*St. Francis of Assisi (1182–1226)*

Remember that when you leave this earth, you can take with you nothing that you have received—only what you have given: a full heart enriched by honest service, love, sacrifice and courage.
—*St. Francis of Assisi (1182–1226)*

Regardless of danger, I must make known the gift of God. . . . Without fear I must spread everywhere the name of God, so that after my death I may leave a bequest to my brethren and sons whom I have baptized in the Lord. —*St. Patrick (c. 385–461)*

Let them do good, and be rich in well-doing. Be ready to give generously and share with others.
— *I Timothy 6:18 (REB)*

He that gives his heart will not deny his money. —*Thomas Fuller (1654–1734)*

Deeds of giving are the very foundation of the world. —*Torah*

'Tis much better to give than to receive—and it's deductible. —*Unknown*

Thank the Lord that you can give, instead of depending on others to give to you. —*Unknown*

Give to every other human being every right that you claim for yourself—that is my doctrine.
— *Thomas Paine (1737–1809)*

When some people give their old clothes to charity, they should stay in them. —*Unknown*

When the heart is converted, the purse is inverted. —*Unknown*

Giving honors the giver. —*Unknown*

May God forbid that we should present our gifts and withhold ourselves. —*Unknown*

Giving should be based on principle, regulated by system, beautified by self-sacrifice. —*Unknown*

Giving until it hurts is not a true measure of charity. Some are more easily hurt than others. —*Unknown*

True giving finds its basis in honest humility and respect. It meets real needs without regard to our own. —*Unknown*

Who gives me a little gift, he wishes that I live. —*Unknown*

It's not what you'd do with a million,
If riches should e'er be your lot;
But what are you doing at present
With a dollar and quarter you've got?
—*Unknown*

Don't be afraid of giving. You can never give too much, if you are giving willingly. —*Unknown*

Don't give until it hurts. Give until it feels good! —*Unknown*

The Lord loves a cheerful giver, and so does everyone else. —*Unknown*

You haven't begun to give until you feel glad over it. —*Unknown*

If truth takes possession of a man's heart, it will direct his hand to his pocketbook. —*Unknown*

We get from people what we give;
We find in them what we bring;
We discover that the changes in them are really changes in ourselves.
—*Unknown*

The man who takes and never gives, may last for years but never lives. —*Unknown*

Everyone must be a giver. It is essential to life. —*Unknown*

If you want to be rich, give! If you want to be poor, grasp! —*Unknown*

Lord, make me willing
To give what I cannot keep,
To gain what I cannot lose.
—*Unknown*

The open hand of giving is always full. —*Unknown*

Give a man a fish and he will eat for a day. Teach him how to fish and he will eat for the rest of his life.
—*Unknown*

Give not from the top of your purse but from the bottom of your heart. —*Unknown*

Contributing to a meaningful cause does not slow down life's pace, but it does make it more tolerable.
—*Unknown*

Most altruistic gift: an anonymous donor giving to an unknown recipient of some future generation.
—*Unknown*

The heart that gives gathers. —*Unknown*

Help us to give according to our incomes, lest Thou, O God, make our incomes according to our gifts.
—*Unknown*

From the first gift that was ever given, right up to this day the basic and fundamental reason for giving has been to fill a need. People give from the heart, not from economics. When a need is recognized, the heart moves with the hand. —*Unknown*

There's a great joy in my giving. It's thrilling. It's exhilarating. It's important to be a part of sharing. It is my love. It is my joy. —*W. Clement Stone (1902-)*

When I give, I give myself. —*Walt Whitman (1819–1892)*

Exhaling is necessary to physical health; giving is essential to spiritual health.
—*William Arthur Ward (1921-)*

We can fill each day with grasping or with giving; with griping or with gratitude.
—*William Arthur Ward (1921-)*

The momentary thrill of getting rarely equals the lasting joy of giving. —*William Arthur Ward (1921-)*

There is no greater joy under the sun than the joy of giving: giving of one's time, energy, talent, and money to help one's fellow man. —*William H. Taylor (1920-)*

There are three kicks in every dollar. One when you make it. One when you save it. One when you give it away. And the last is the biggest of all. —*William Allen White (1868–1944)*

Give all thou canst; high Heaven rejects the lore of nicely-calculated less or more. —*William Wordsworth (1770–1850)*

We make a living by what we get, but we make a life by what we give. —*Winston Churchill (1874–1965)*

❧

HAPPINESS

**Cheer • Gladness • Gratitude
Joy • Satisfaction**

Happiness adds and multiplies as we divide it with others. —*A. Nielsen (1897–1980)*

Most folks are about as happy as they make up their minds to be. —*Abraham Lincoln (1809–1865)*

What can be added to the happiness of a man who is in health, out of debt, and has a clear conscience?
—*Adam Smith (1723–1790)*

Happiness is nothing more than health and a poor memory. —*Albert Schweitzer (1875–1965)*

To pursue joy is to lose it. The only way to get it is to follow steadily the path of duty.
—*Alexander MacLaren (1826–1910)*

The hand that in life grips with a miser's clutch, and the ear that refuses to heed the pleading voice of humanity forfeit the most precious of all gifts of earth and of heaven—the happiness that comes of doing good to others. —*Amon G. Carter, Jr. (1919–1982)*

The secret of happiness is renunciation. —*Andrew Carnegie (1835–1919)*

There is no happiness for people at the expense of other people. —*Anwar el-Sadat (1918–1981)*

He who has health has hope; and he who has hope has everything. —*Arabian Proverb*

If you want to have a happy life, take up giving as a hobby when you're young.
—*Arthur F. Lenehan (1921-)*

Happiness is the legitimate fruitage of love and service. —*Arthur S. Hardy (1847–1930)*

The human being who lives only for himself finally reaps nothing but unhappiness. Unselfishness corrodes. Unselfishness ennobles, satisfies. Don't put off the joy derivable from doing helpful, kindly things for others. —*B. C. Forbes (1880–1954)*

We must learn that to enjoy happiness we must conscientiously and continuously seek to spread happiness. Selfishness is suicidal to happiness. —*B. C. Forbes (1880–1954)*

Business was originated to produce happiness, not to pile up millions. —*B. C. Forbes (1880–1954)*

The health of the people is really the foundation upon which all their happiness and all their powers as a state depend. —*Benjamin Disraeli (1804–1881)*

I know that unless I'm true to myself I couldn't be happy. Too much emphasis is placed today on externals and too little on character. —*Betty White (1924-)*

In proportion as one loses himself in [a great cause]. . .in the same degree does he get the highest happiness out of his work. —*Booker T. Washington (1856–1915)*

Happiness is, in the end, a simple thing. . . . Happiness is really caring and being able to do something about the caring. —*Brian O'Connell (1930-)*

Your own happiness increases the more you give your happiness away. —*Bruce Bogaert (1934-)*

You've got to get up every morning with a smile on your face, and show the world all the love in your heart. —*Carole King (1942-)*

Happiness is a way station between too little and too much. —*Channing Pollock (1880–1946)*

Reflect upon your present blessings of which every man has many; not upon your past misfortunes of which all have some. —*Charles Dickens (1812–1870)*

Good humor and enthusiasm should be the sunshine ahead that will keep that shadow behind. —*Charles Field (1836–1912)*

The most useless day is that in which we have not laughed. —*Charles Field (1836–1912)*

It is not how much we have, but how much we enjoy, that makes happiness. —*Charles H. Spurgeon (1834–1892)*

We act as though comfort and luxury were the chief requirements of life, when all that we need to make us really happy is something to be enthusiastic about. —*Charles Kingsley (1819–1875)*

Happiness quite unshared can scarcely be called happiness; it has no taste.
—*Charlotte Bronte (1816–1855)*

To attain happiness in another world we need only to believe something, while to secure it in this world, we must do something. —*Charlotte Perkins Gilman (1860–1935)*

One joy scatters a hundred griefs. —*Chinese Proverb*

Remember happiness doesn't depend upon who you are or what you have; it depends solely upon what you think. —*Dale Carnegie (1888–1955)*

Contentment is the realization of how much I already have. —*Dave Grant (1939-)*

Happiness is a by product of what we share with others. —*Douglas M. Lawson (1936-)*

If we'd only stop trying to be happy, we could have a pretty good time. —*Edith Wharton (1862–1937)*

To be happy, you must forget yourself. Learn benevolence. —*Edward Bulwer-Lytton (1803–1873)*

You get more joy out of giving joy to others and should put a good deal of thought into the happiness that you are able to give. —*Eleanor Roosevelt (1884–1962)*

Remember that not to be happy is not to be grateful. —*Elizabeth Carter (1717–1806)*

Those who in everything make God first and last and best, are the happiest people in the world.
—*Ellen G. White (1827–1915)*

He is a wise man who does not grieve for the things which he has not, but rejoices for those which he has.
—*Epictetus (50–120)*

You grow up the day you have your first real laugh—at yourself. —*Ethel Barrymore (1879–1959)*

Happiness, it is said, is seldom found by those who seek it, and never by those who seek it for themselves.
—*F. Emerson Andrews (1902–1978)*

Oh, what a happy child I am,
Although I cannot see!
I am resolved that in this world
Contented I will be!
—*Fanny Crosby (1820–1905)*

Happiness lies in the joy of achievement and the thrill of creative effort.
—*Franklin D. Roosevelt (1882–1945)*

There can be no happiness if the things we believe in are different from the things we do.
—*Freya Stark (1893–)*

Employment is nature's physician, and is essential to human happiness. —*Galen (c. 129–199)*

The contented man is never poor; the discontented never rich. —*George Eliot (1819–1880)*

To praise is an investment in happiness. —*George Matthew Adams (1878–1962)*

One is happy as a result of one's own efforts, once one knows the necessary ingredients of happiness:
simple tastes, a certain degree of courage, self-denial to a point, love of work, and above all, a clear
conscience. —*George Sand (1804–1876)*

Continual cheerfulness is a sign of wisdom. —*German Proverb*

The only way to enjoy anything in life is to earn it first. —*Ginger Rogers (1911–)*

Nothing will content him who is not content with a little. —*Greek Proverb*

Happiness is a by-product of an effort to make someone else happy.
—*Gretta Brooker Palmer (1905–1953)*

To be of use in the world is the only way to happiness. —*Hans Christian Andersen (1805–1875)*

Give me neither poverty nor riches, but give me contentment. —*Helen Keller (1880–1968)*

When one door of happiness closes, another opens; but often we look so long at the closed door that we do
not see the one which has been opened for us. —*Helen Keller (1880–1968)*

Many persons have a wrong idea of what constitutes true happiness. It is not attained through self-
gratification but through fidelity to a worthy purpose. —*Helen Keller (1880–1968)*

We make ourselves rich by making our wants few. —*Henry David Thoreau (1817–1862)*

Half of the world is on the wrong scent in the pursuit of happiness. They think it consists in having and getting, and in being served by others. It consists in giving and in serving others.
—*Henry Drummond (1854–1907)*

There is no happiness in having or in getting, but only in giving. —*Henry Drummond (1854–1907)*

Happiness is inward, and not outward; and so it does not depend on what we have, but on what we are.
—*Henry Van Dyke (1852–1933)*

Be glad of life because it gives you the chance to love and to work and to play and to look up at the stars.
—*Henry Van Dyke (1852–1933)*

The world is like a mirror; frown at it, and it frowns at you. Smile, and it smiles, too.
—*Herbert Samuel (1870–1963)*

Some patients, though conscious that their condition is perilous, recover their health simply through their contentment with the goodness of the physician. —*Hippocrates (460–377 B.C.)*

People at my stage of life are apt to cherish the past and be pessimistic about the future. But when I meet energetic young people who are making wonderful contributions to the communities, I feel rejuvenated and full of hope and trust in the future. —*Hirokichi Yoshiyama (1911-)*

Real happiness is cheap enough, yet how dearly we pay for its counterfeit. —*Hosea Ballou (1771–1852)*

A happy person is not a person in a certain set of circumstances, but rather a person with a certain set of attitudes. —*Hugh Downs (1921-)*

The secret of happiness is not in doing what one likes to do, but liking what one has to do.
—*James Matthew Barrie (1860–1937)*

Those who bring sunshine to the lives of others cannot keep it from themselves.
—*James Matthew Barrie (1860–1937)*

Happiness sneaks in through a door you didn't know you left open. —*John Barrymore (1882-1942)*

I am content with what I have, be it little, or much. —*John Bunyan (1628–1688)*

A joy that's shared is a joy made double. —*John Ray (1627–1705)*

I will strive to raise my own body and soul daily into all the higher powers of duty and happiness, not in rivalship or contention with others but for the help and delight and honor of others and for the joy and peace of my own life. —*John Ruskin (1819–1900)*

A contented mind is the greatest blessing a man can enjoy in this world. —*Joseph Addison (1672–1719)*

The grand essentials to happiness in this life are something to do, something to love, and something to hope for. —*Joseph Addison (1672–1719)*

Not what we have, but what we use, not what we see, but what we choose, these are the things that mar or bless the sum of happiness. —*Joseph Fort Newton (1878–1949)*

Don't mistake pleasure for happiness. They are a different breed of dogs. —*Josh Billings (1818–1885)*

The best we can do is to go through life trying to be happy and helping those we meet along the way.
—*Kate Smith (1909–1986)*

It's pretty hard to tell what brings happiness; poverty and wealth have both failed.
—*Ken Hubbard (1868–1930)*

The purpose of life is not to be happy. The purpose of life is to matter, to be productive, to have it make some difference that you live at all. —*Leo Rosten (1908-)*

Joy can be real only if people look upon their life as a service, and have a definite object in life outside themselves and their personal happiness. —*Leo Tolstoy (1828–1910)*

The only certain happiness in life is to live for others. —*Leo Tolstoy (1828–1910)*

Buried deep in the maze of commonplace, the pearl of true happiness lies. And he who rejoices in little things, finds the pathway that leads to the prize. —*Lucy M. Thompson (1856–?)*

Very little is needed to make a happy life. It is all within yourself, in your way of thinking.
—*Marcus Aurelius Antoninus (121–180)*

To be content with little is difficult; to be content with much, impossible.
—*Marie Ebner von Eschenbach (1830–1916)*

The greater part of our happiness or misery depends on our disposition and not our circumstances.
—*Martha Washington (1731 –1802)*

Laughter is taken as a sign of strength, freedom, health, beauty, youth, and happiness.
—*Martin Grotjahn (1904-)*

Those who are not looking for happiness are the most likely to find it, because those who are searching forget that the surest way to be happy is to seek happiness for others. —*Martin Luther (1483–1546)*

Blessed is he who submits to the will of God; he can never be unhappy. —*Martin Luther (1483–1546)*

Every day I live I am more convinced that the waste of life lies in the love we have not given, the powers we have not used, the selfish prudence that will risk nothing and which, shirking pain, misses happiness as well. —*Mary Cholmondeley (1859–1925)*

Happiness is like a butterfly, which, when pursued, is always just beyond your grasp, but which, if you will sit down quietly, may alight upon you. —*Nathaniel Hawthorne (1804–1864)*

To feel good about yourself do this . . . start giving. Give yourself to someone in some service that you do not need to give. Just let yourself flow out to people. This will make you feel awfully good about yourself. —*Norman Vincent Peale (1898–1993)*

Happiness will never come if it's a goal in itself; happiness is a by-product of a commitment of worthy causes. —*Norman Vincent Peale (1898–1993)*

Be too large for worry, too noble for anger, too strong for fear and too happy to permit the presence of trouble. —*Optimists' Creed*

The true source of cheerfulness is benevolence. The soul that perpetually overflows with kindness and sympathy will always be cheerful. —*Parke Godwin (1816–1904)*

For I have learned, in whatsoever state I am, therewith to be content. —*Philippians 4:11*

Hope deferred makes the heart sick, but a longing fulfilled is a tree of life. —*Proverbs 13:12*

He that hath mercy on the poor, happy is he. —*Proverbs 14:21*

A cheerful heart is a good medicine, but a downcast spirit dries up the bones. —*Proverbs 17:22 (RSV)*

Happiness is not having what you want, but wanting what you have.
—*Rabbi Hyman Schachtel (1907-)*

There is no beautifier of complexion, or form, or behavior, like the wish to scatter joy and not pain around us. —*Ralph Waldo Emerson (1803–1882)*

Joy is not in things; it is in us. —*Richard Wagner (1813–1883)*

Happiness is the only good. The time to be happy is now. The place to be happy is here. The way to be happy is to make others so. —*Robert G. Ingersoll (1833–1899)*

The time to be happy is now. The place to be happy is here. The way to be happy is to make others so. —*Robert G. Ingersoll (1833–1899)*

Look at what you have left not at what you have lost. —*Robert H. Schuller (1926-)*

Happiness, at least is not solitary; it joys to communicate; it loves others, for it depends on them for its existence. —*Robert Louis Stevenson (1850–1894)*

There is no duty we underrate so much as the duty of being happy.
—*Robert Louis Stevenson (1850–1894)*

Share the happiness of those who are happy, and the sorrow of those who are sad.
—*Romans 12:15 (P)*

When someone does something good, applaud! You'll make two people happy.
—*Samuel Goldwyn (1882–1974)*

Happiness is the sense that one matters. Happiness is an abiding enthusiasm. Happiness is single-mindedness. Happiness is whole-heartedness. Happiness is a by-product. Happiness is faith.
—*Samuel M. Shoemaker (1893–1963)*

For yesterday is but a memory and tomorrow is only a vision; but today well lived makes every yesterday a memory of happiness and every tomorrow a vision of hope. —*Sanskrit Poem*

There is no greater joy nor greater reward than to make a fundamental difference in someone's life.
—*Sister Mary Rose McGeady (1928-)*

Shared joy is double joy and shared sorrow is half-sorrow. —*Swedish Proverb*

Happy is he who performs a good deed: for he may tip the scales for himself and the world. —*The Talmud*

Happiness comes only with labor and effort and self-sacrifice, and from those whose joy in life springs in part from power of work and sense of duty. —*Theodore Roosevelt (1858–1919)*

Happiness is never a goal to be pursued. It is always the unexpected surprise of a life lived in service to others. —*Tom Sine*

It is difficult for any of us to go through life without either increasing or diminishing somebody's happiness. —*Unknown*

Now and then it's good to pause in our pursuit of happiness and just be happy. —*Unknown*

It is not what we have but what we enjoy that makes happiness. —*Unknown*

The way to be happy is to make others happy. —*Unknown*

True happiness comes from the knowledge that we are of some use in this world. —*Unknown*

True happiness, it has been well said, is not to be found in more possessions, or in the expenditure of wealth for the physical things of life. True happiness will be found, as it ever has been, in the deep satisfaction that comes from contributing to worthwhile community needs. —*Unknown*

Who lives content with little possesses everything. —*Unknown*

Happiness is like a kiss—in order to get any good out of it you have to give it to somebody else. —*Unknown*

You can't pursue happiness and catch it. Happiness comes upon you unaware while you are helping others. —*Unknown*

There is no greater happiness than that which comes from sharing . . . no greater joy than that which comes from loving, giving, and caring. —*Unknown*

You will be happier if you will give people a bit of your heart rather than a piece of your mind. —*Unknown*

The only true happiness is that which we give others. —*Unknown*

Three things make us happy and content: the seeing eye, the hearing ear, the responsive heart. —*Unknown*

There is no real lasting joy in self-seeking. —*Victor Collins (1913-)*

The supreme happiness of life is the conviction that we are loved. —*Victor Hugo (1802–1885)*

Man is not on the earth solely for his own happiness. He is there to realize great things for humanity. —*Vincent van Gogh (1853–1890)*

There is no way to happiness—happiness is the way. —*Wayne Dyer (1940-)*

Real joy comes not from ease or riches or from the praise of men, but from doing something worthwhile. —*Sir Wilfred Grenfell (1865–1940)*

That is happiness: to be dissolved into something completely great. —*Willa Cather (1873–1947)*

The roots of happiness grow deepest in the soil of service. —*William Arthur Ward (1921-)*

The surest cure for loneliness, the quickest way to happiness, is found in this, a simple creed: Go serve someone in greater need. —*William Arthur Ward (1921-)*

Happiness is not dependent upon circumstances but upon attitudes; it is not so much environmental as mental. —*William Arthur Ward (1921-)*

Existence is a strange bargain. Life owes us little; we owe it everything. The only true happiness comes from squandering ourselves for a purpose. —*William Cowper (1731–1800)*

Be happy with what you have and are, be generous with both, and you won't have to hunt for happiness. —*William Gladstone (1809–1898)*

True happiness, if understood, consists alone in doing good. —*William Somerville (1682–1742)*

The happiest people I know are those who have learned to live beyond their own special interests by discovering the rewards that come from giving of themselves. —*Winfield C. Dunn (1927)*

Doing good to others is not a duty. It is a joy, for it increases your own health and happiness. —*Zoroastrian Scriptures*

❦

KINDNESS
Benevolence • Kindhearted • Benign
Compassion • Thoughtfulness

If you have not often felt the joy of doing a kind act, you have neglected much, and most of all yourself.
—*A. Nielsen (1897–1980)*

All the gold in the world has no significance. That which is lasting are the thoughtful acts which we do for our fellow man. —*Adolfo Prieto (1867–1945)*

No act of kindness, no matter how small, is ever wasted. —*Aesop (620-560 B.C.)*

Man is here for the sake of other men—for those upon whose smile and well-being our own happiness depends, and also for the countless unknown souls with whose fate we are connected by a bond of sympathy. —*Albert Einstein (1879–1955)*

All people are endowed with the faculty of compassion, and for this reason can develop the humanitarian spirit. —*Albert Schweitzer (1875–1965)*

Teach me to feel another's woe,
To hide the fault I see:
That mercy I to others show,
That mercy show to me.
—*Alexander Pope (1688–1744)*

The kindness of the American people is, so far as I know, something unique in the history of the world.
—*Alfred North Whitehead (1861–1947)*

There is nothing so kingly as kindness. —*Alice Cary (1820–1871)*

Be kind, generous and loving in your thoughts, words and actions. —*Ann Sykes Walter (1915–1981)*

If you think of your fellow creatures, then you only want to cry; you could really cry the whole day long. The only thing to do is to pray that God will perform a miracle . . . and I hope that I am doing enough of that! —*Anne Frank (1929–1945)*

Practice random kindness and senseless acts of beauty. —*Anne Herbert (1952-)*

Make no judgments where you have no compassion. —*Anne McCaffrey (1926-)*

Compassion is the basis of all morality. —*Arthur Schopenhauer (1788–1860)*

The size of your body is of little account; the size of your brain is of much account; the size of your heart is of the most account of all. —*B. C. Forbes (1880–1954)*

It doesn't matter who or where you are, or how successful you become in a worldly way . . . in a corporate board room, in a hospital operating theater, setting public policy, or managing your private life . . . you must care for other people. —*Barbara Bush (1925-)*

Kind words do not cost much. They never blister the tongue or lips. They make other people good-natured. They also produce their own image on men's souls, and a beautiful image it is.
—*Blaise Pascal (1623–1662)*

Noble deeds that are concealed are most esteemed. —*Blaise Pascal (1623–1662)*

Certain beliefs must accompany every action: One should act without selfishness, cultivate compassion for all living things, and develop respect for others. —*Bstan'dzin-rgya-mtsho (1935-)*

Kindness is the evidence of greatness. If anyone is glad that you are here, then you have not lived in vain.
—*Charles Fenno Hoffman (1806–1884)*

Never, if possible, lie down at night without being able to say: I have made one human being, at least, a little wiser, a little happier, or a little better this day. —*Charles Kingsley (1819–1875)*

Don't think too much about yourself. Try to cultivate the habit of thinking of others; this will reward you.
—*Charles W. Eliot (1834–1926)*

A kind word warms for three winters. —*Chinese Proverb*

The small courtesies sweeten life; the greater ennoble it. —*Christian Nestell Bovee (1820–1904)*

Consideration for others is the basis of a good life, a good society. —*Confucius (551–479 B.C.)*

He who sees a need and waits to be asked for help is as unkind as if he had refused it.
—*Dante Alighieri (1265–1321)*

There is no such thing as an insignificant human being. To treat people that way is a kind of sin and there's no reason for it. None. —*Debbi Fields (1957–)*

Sharing with others is caring for others in action. —*Douglas M. Lawson (1936–)*

Do unto others as though you were the others. —*Elbert Hubbard (1856–1915)*

We are weaving character every day, and the way to weave the best character is to be kind and to be useful. Think right, act right; it is what we think and do that makes us what we are.
—*Elbert Hubbard (1856–1915)*

So many gods, so many creeds, so many paths that wind and wind. When just the art of being kind is all this sad world needs. —*Ella Wheeler Wilcox (1855–1919)*

To be a complete person is to be a part of others, and share a part of them. —*Elliot Richardson (1920–)*

Be kind and compassionate to one another, forgiving each other. . . . —*Ephesians 4:32 (NIV)*

Kind words are the music of the world. —*Frederick William Faber (1814–1863)*

Compassion is the chief law of human existence. —*Feodor Dostoevski (1821–1881)*

Don't be misled; remember that you can't ignore God and get away with it: a man will always reap just the kind of crop he sows! —*Galatians 6:7 (LB)*

Am I my brother's keeper? —*Genesis 4:9*

In scattering seeds of kindness, do it by hand and not by machine. —*George Ade (1866–1944)*

As Americans, our purpose is to make kinder the face of the nation and gentler the face of the world.
—*George Bush (1924–)*

May every soul that touches mine—be it the slightest contact—get there from some good; some little grace; one kindly thought; one aspiration yet unfelt; one bit of courage for the darkening sky; one gleam of faith to brave the thickening ills of life; one glimpse of brighter skies beyond the gathering mists—to make this life worthwhile. —*George Eliot (1819–1880)*

The dew of compassion is a tear. —*George Gordon Byron (1788–1824)*

Guard within yourself that treasure, kindness. Know how to give without hesitation, how to lose without regret, how to acquire without meanness. —*George Sand (1804–1876)*

Real unselfishness consists in sharing the interests of others. —*George Santayana (1863–1952)*

Perhaps the world little notes nor long remembers individual acts of kindness—but people do. —*H. Albright (1928-)*

Kindness is the beginning and the end of the law. —*Hebrew Proverb*

Never neglect to show kindness and to share what you have with others; for such are the sacrifices which God approves. —*Hebrews 13:16 (REV)*

Compassion is born when we discover in the center of our own existence not only that God is God and man is man, but also that our neighbor really is our fellow man. —*Henri Nouwen (1932-)*

It is not genius, nor glory, nor love that reflects the greatness of the human soul; it is kindness. —*Henri-Dominique Lacordaire*

There is a loftier ambition than merely to stand high in the world. It is to stoop down and lift mankind a little higher. —*Henry Van Dyke (1852–1933)*

He that planteth a tree . . . provideth a kindness for many generations. —*Henry Van Dyke (1852–1933)*

Do not keep the alabaster boxes of your love and tenderness sealed up until your friends are dead. Fill their lives with sweetness. Speak approving, cheering words while their ears can hear them and while their hearts can be thrilled by them. —*Henry Ward Beecher (1813–1887)*

He who does kind deeds becomes rich. —*Hindu Proverb*

I led them with cords of compassion, with bands of love. —*Hosea 11:4 (RSV)*

Life is made up, not of great sacrifices or duties, but of little things, in which smiles, and kindnesses, and small obligations, given habitually, are what win and preserve the heart and secure comfort. —*Humphrey Davy (1778–1829)*

True compassion is walking in the shoes of those who have no feet. —*Jackie A. Strange (1927-)*

He who distributes the milk of human kindness cannot help but spill a little on himself.
—*James Matthew Barrie (1860–1937)*

One kind word can warm three winter months. —*Japanese Proverb*

What wisdom can you find that is greater than kindness? —*Jean-Jacques Rousseau (1712–1778)*

Stand for something—have passion and compassion for something larger than yourself. Care greater and deeper about others. —*Jerold Panas (1932-)*

He who prays for his neighbor will be heard for himself. —*Jewish Proverb*

Sympathy doesn't provide food, but it makes hunger more endurable. —*Jewish Proverb*

Sympathy is a little medicine to soothe the ache in another's heart. —*Jewish Proverb*

Kindness is the golden chain by which society is bound together.
—*Johann Wolfgang von Goethe (1749–1832)*

If I accept you as you are, I will make you worse; however, if I treat you as though you are what you are capable of becoming, I help you become that. —*Johann Wolfgang von Goethe (1749–1832)*

A part of kindness consists in loving people more than they deserve. —*Joseph Joubert (1754–1824)*

Little deeds of kindness,
Little words of love,
Help to make earth happy,
Like the heaven above.
—*Julia A. Carney (1823–1908)*

I have learned silence from the talkative; tolerance from the intolerant; and kindness from the unkind.
—*Kahlil Gibran (1883–1931)*

It is of the Lord's mercies that we are not consumed, because his compassion fails not.
—*Lamentations 3:22*

Kindness in words creates confidence. Kindness in thinking creates profoundness. Kindness in giving creates love. —*Lao-tzu (604–531 B.C.)*

The older you get, the more you realize that kindness is synonymous with happiness.
—*Lionel Barrymore (1878–1954)*

Politeness is an easy virtue, costs little, and has great purchasing power.
—*Louisa May Alcott (1832–1888)*

I had rather never receive a kindness than never bestow one.
—*Lucius Annaeus Seneca (4 B.C.–A.D. 65)*

The man with two tunics should share with him who has none, and the one who has food should do the same. —*Luke 3:11 (NIV)*

One can pay back the loan of gold, but one dies forever in debt to those who are kind.
—*Malayan Proverb*

Tears may be dried up, but the heart never. —*Marguerite de Valois (1553–1615)*

Kindness is a language which the deaf can hear and the blind can see. —*Mark Twain (1835–1910)*

If you stop to be kind, you must swerve often from your path. —*Mary Webb (1881–1927)*

Therefore all things whatsoever ye would that men should do to you, do ye even so to them.
—*Matthew 7:12*

Great people are able to do great kindnesses. —*Miguel de Cervantes (1547–1616)*

Kind words can be short and easy to speak, but their echoes are truly endless. —*Mother Teresa (1910-)*

Let us more and more insist on raising funds of love, of kindness, of understanding, of peace. . . . The rest will be given. —*Mother Teresa (1910-)*

I would rather make mistakes in kindness and compassion than work miracles in unkindness and hardness. —*Mother Teresa (1910-)*

Be kind and merciful. Let no one ever come to you without leaving better and happier.
—*Mother Teresa (1910-)*

The capacity to care is the thing that gives life its deepest meaning and significance.
—*Pablo Casals (1876–1973)*

With a sweet tongue and kindness, you can drag an elephant by a hair. —*Persian Proverb*

Let everyone see that you are unselfish and considerate in all you do. —*Philippians 4:5 (LB)*

Be kind, for everyone you meet is fighting a hard battle. —*Philo Judaeus c. (20 B.C.– A.D. 50)*

Never hesitate to hold out your hand; never hesitate to accept the outstretched hand of another.
—*Pope John XXIII (1881–1963)*

Your own soul is nourished when you are kind; it is destroyed when you are cruel. —*Proverbs 11:17*

He who oppresses the poor shows contempt for their Maker, but whoever is kind to the needy honors God.
—*Proverbs 14:31 (NIV)*

Never tire of loyalty and kindness. Hold these virtues tightly. Write them deep within your heart.
—*Proverbs 3:3 (LB)*

He that hath pity upon the poor lendeth unto the Lord; and that which he hath given will he pay him again. —*Proverbs 19:17*

He who has a bountiful eye will be blessed, for he shares his bread with the poor. —*Proverbs 22:9*

He hath made His wonderful works to be remembered: The Lord is gracious and full of compassion.
—*Psalms 111:4*

Your goodness and unfailing kindness shall be with me all of my life. . . . —*Psalms 23:6 (LB)*

O Lord: let thy loving kindness and thy truth continually preserve me. —*Psalms 40:11*

Kindness is a hard thing to give away. It keeps coming back to the giver. —*Ralph Scott (1921-)*

You cannot do a kindness too soon because you never know how soon it will be too late.
—*Ralph Waldo Emerson (1803–1882)*

There is a world of practical religion in simply being considerate of others.
—*Roger Babson (1875–1967)*

Our country is great because it is built on principles of self-reliance, opportunity, innovation, and compassion for others. —*Ronald Reagan (1911-)*

We must bring compassion back to the market place. Social justice is our goal. To achieve it, we all must help create a more tolerant and fair society. —*Rose Bird (1936-)*

The good that men do lives after them. —*Ruth Gordon (1896–1985)*

To cultivate kindness is a valuable part of the business life. —*Samuel Johnson (1709–1784)*

As in filling a vessel drop by drop, there is at last a drop which makes it run over; so it is in a series of kindnesses, there is at last one which makes the heart run over. —*Samuel Johnson (1709–1784)*

The most effective public official is one who, while finding passage through the maze of economic and governmental considerations, never forgets that compassion for people comes first.
—*Shirley Pettis Roberson (1924-)*

Kindness gives birth to kindness. —*Sophocles (495–406 B.C.)*

'Tis better to be known as a good man than a great one, for greatness is an assessment of mortals; goodness a gift of God. —*Spark Matsunaga (1916–1990)*

As small as it may seem, a good deed is always worth the doing. —*Spark Matsunaga (1916–1990)*

I expect to pass through this world but once. Any good or any kindness that I can show to my fellow creature, let me do it now, for I shall not pass this way again. —*Stephen Grellet (1773–1855)*

Too much has been said of the heroes of history—the strong men, the troublesome men; too little of the amiable, the kindly and the tolerant. —*Stephen Leacock (1869–1944)*

Loving kindness is greater than laws; and the charities of life are more than all ceremonies.
—*The Talmud*

The man who asks mercy for another while both are in peril will be answered first. —*The Talmud*

Have therefore, compassion in your hearts, my children, because even as a man doeth to his neighbor, even so also will the Lord do to him. —*The Twelve Testaments-Zebulun*

Let me urge that we keep clear of two besetting sins—hardness of heart and softness of head.
—*Theodore Roosevelt (1858–1919)*

Man should not consider his material possessions his own, but as common to all, so as to share them without hesitation when others are in need. —*Thomas Aquinas (1225–1274)*

Without kindness there can be no true joy. —*Thomas Carlyle (1795–1881)*

Our deeds are like stones cast into the pool of time; though they themselves may disappear, their ripples extend to eternity. —*Unknown*

It's not the difference between people that's the difficulty. It's the indifference. —*Unknown*

Compassion is our way of sharing the pain of others. —*Unknown*

Compassion is your pain in my heart. —*Unknown*

The true measure of a man is the height of his ideals, the breadth of his sympathy, the depth of his convictions, and the length of his patience. —*Unknown*

It should not discourage us if our kindness is unacknowledged; it has its influence still. —*Unknown*

Gratitude is the music of the heart, when its chords are swept by the breeze of kindness. —*Unknown*

Kindness is like snow; it makes everything it covers beautiful. —*Unknown*

Kindness is something you have received and have to pass on in order to keep it. —*Unknown*

Kindness is the oil that takes friction out of life. —*Unknown*

Kindness may be achieved by all, rich and poor, learned and illiterate. Brilliance of mind and capacity for deep thinking have rendered great service to humanity, but by themselves they are impotent to dry a tear or mend a broken heart. —*Unknown*

There is a vast difference between putting your nose in other people's business and putting your heart in other people's problems. —*Unknown*

Never lose an opportunity of saying a kind word nor of doing a kind act. —*Unknown*

We're put on this earth not to see through each other but to see each other through. —*Unknown*

Sympathy is two hearts tugging at the same load. —*Unknown*

Sympathy sees, and says, 'I'm sorry.' Compassion feels, and whispers, 'I'll help.' —*Unknown*

Take the time to understand and lend a gentle helping hand. —*Unknown*

Loving-kindness is the better part of goodness. —*W. Somerset Maugham (1874–1965)*

Unconcern asks: 'Am I my brother's keeper?' Compassion proclaims: 'I am my neighbor's brother!' —*William Arthur Ward (1921-)*

Be considerate—you may need help yourself some day. —*William Feather (1870–1944)*

This is the final test of a gentleman: his respect for those who can be of no possible service to him. —*William Lyon Phelps (1865–1943)*

We are here not to get all we can out of life for ourselves, but to try to make the lives of others happier.
—*William Osler (1849–1919)*

I expect to pass through life but once. If therefore, there be any kindness I can show, or any good thing I can do to any fellow being, let me do it now, and not defer or neglect it, as I shall not pass this way again.
—*William Penn (1644–1718)*

The best portion of a good man's life is his little, nameless, unremembered acts of kindness and of love.
—*William Wordsworth (1770–1850)*

Administer true justice; show mercy and compassion to one another. —*Zechariah 7:9 (NIV)*

The greatest good we can do for others is not just to share our riches with them, but to reveal theirs.
—*Zig Ziglar (1926-)*

LEADERSHIP

Guidance • Servant-Leadership • Administration
Direction • Management

Great necessities call forth great leaders. —*Abigail Adams (1744–1818)*

There are many elements to a campaign. Leadership is number one. Everything else is number two. —*Bernd Brecher (1932-)*

Leaders don't force people to follow—they invite them on a journey. —*Charles S. Lauer (1930-)*

Leadership is action, not position. —*Donald H. McGannon (1920–1984)*

Leadership: the art of getting someone else to do something you want done because he wants to do it. —*Dwight D. Eisenhower (1890–1969)*

No organization is stronger than the quality of its leadership, or ever extends its constituency far beyond the degree to which its leadership is representative. —*Edgar Powell (1922–1984)*

A good leader can't get too far ahead of his followers. —*Franklin D. Roosevelt (1882–1945)*

When the leadership is right and the time is right, the people can always be counted upon to follow—to the end and at all costs. —*Harold J. Seymour (1894–1968)*

Leaders are the ones who keep faith with the past, keep step with the present, and keep the promise to posterity. —*Harold J. Seymour (1894–1968)*

Have no illusions about the power of money; but it is silly to dismiss it as worthless. It is not. It means many good things. It represents dormitories, classrooms, hospitals. It represents research facilities and the priceless efforts of men and women of creative skill and genius. But money alone cannot build character or transform evil into good . . . It cries for full partnership with leaders of character and goodwill who value good tools in the creation and enlargement of life for man, who is created in the image of God.
—*Howard C. Baldwin*

Leadership is the special quality which enables people to stand up and pull the rest of us over the horizon.
—*James L. Fisher (1931-)*

The main characteristics of effective leadership are intelligence, integrity or loyalty, mystique, humor, discipline, courage, self sufficiency and confidence. —*James L. Fisher (1931-)*

Be gentle and you can be bold; be frugal and you can be liberal; avoid putting yourself before others and you can become a leader among men. —*Lao-tzu (604–531 B.C.)*

A leader is best when people barely know he exists, not so good when people obey and acclaim him, worse when they despise him . . . . But of a good leader who talks little when his work is done, his aim fulfilled, they will say, "We did it ourselves." —*Lao-tzu (604–531 B.C.)*

Leadership should be born out of the understanding of the needs of those who would be affected by it.
—*Marian Anderson (1902-)*

Leadership should be more participative than directive, more enabling than performing.
—*Mary D. Poole (1931-)*

There is nothing more difficult to carry out, nor more doubtful of success, nor more dangerous to handle, than to initiate a new order of things.

For the reformer has enemies all who profit by the old order, and only lukewarm defenders in all those who would profit by the new order.

This lukewarmness arises partly from fear of their adversaries who have the law in their favor; and partly from the incredulity of mankind, who do not truly believe in anything new until they have had actual experience of it. —*Niccolo Machiavelli (1469–1527)*

Leadership is not magnetic personality—that can just as well be a glib tongue. It is not "making friends and influencing people"—that is flattery. Leadership is lifting a person's vision to higher sights, the raising of a person's performance to a higher standard, the building of a personality beyond its normal limitations. —*Peter Drucker*

American philanthropic custom owes much to leadership by business and professional people.
—*Robert L. Payton (1926-)*

The only test of leadership is that somebody follows. —*Robert K. Greenleaf (1904-1990)*

Behind every great achievement is a dreamer of great dreams. —*Robert K. Greenleaf (1904-1990)*

Blessed is the leader who considers leadership an opportunity for service. —*Unknown*

The best way to get something done is to begin. —*Unknown*

Blessed is the leader who has not sought the high places, but who has been drafted into service because of his ability and willingness to serve. —*Unknown*

Blessed is the leader who seeks the best for those he serves. —*Unknown*

A good leader inspires others with confidence in him; a great leader inspires them with confidence in themselves. —*Unknown*

Leadership is one of the highest forms of service. It is best exercised when it freely motivates others to a decision that is really theirs—but which may never have been reached without the leader's beneficial influence. —*Unknown*

The final test of a leader is that he leaves behind him in other men the conviction and the will to carry on. —*Walter Lippmann (1889–1974)*

LIFE

**Existence • Living • Character
Growth • Purpose**

The ideals which have lighted my way, and time after time given me new courage to face life cheerfully, have been kindness, beauty, and truth. —_Albert Einstein (1879–1955)_

Only a life lived for others is a life worthwhile. —_Albert Einstein (1879–1955)_

Example is not the main thing in influencing others. It is the only thing.
—_Albert Schweitzer (1875–1965)_

The slightest breeze that ever blew
Some slender grass has wavered;
The smallest life I ever knew
Some other life has flavored.
—_Angela Morgan (1873–1957)_

Life is a team sport. Sometimes you give and sometimes you get. —_Ann Pearson (1945-)_

Use life to provide something that outlasts it. —_B. C. Forbes (1880–1954)_

Remember that wherever our life touches yours, we help or hinder . . . wherever your life touches ours, you make us stronger or weaker. . . . There is no escape—man drags man down, or man lifts man up.
—_Booker T. Washington (1856–1915)_

There is no power on earth that can neutralize the influence of a high, pure, simple, and useful life.
—_Booker T. Washington (1856–1915)_

Simplicity is making the journey of this life with just baggage enough.
—*Charles Dudley Warner (1829–1900)*

Men cannot for long live hopefully unless they are embarked upon some great unifying enterprise—one for which they may pledge their lives, their fortunes and their honor.
—*Clarence Addison Dykstra (1883–1950)*

Be life long or short, its completeness depends on what it was lived for.
—*David Starr Jordan (1851–1931)*

I don't know if I should care for a man who made life easy; I should want someone who made it interesting. —*Edith Wharton (1862–1937)*

Let the moment come when nothing is left but life, and you will find that you do not hesitate over the fate of material possessions. —*Edward von Rickenbacker (1890–1973)*

Live simply that others may simply live. —*Elizabeth Seton (1774–1821)*

He who has a Why to live for can bear almost any How. —*Friedrich Wilhelm Nietzsche (1844–1900)*

If we treat people as they are, they will stay as they are. But if we treat them for what they might be, and might become, they will become those better selves. —*G. T. Smith (1935-)*

My life belongs to the whole community, and as long as I live it is my privilege to do for it whatever I can.
—*George Bernard Shaw (1856–1950)*

It is not well for a man to pray, cream; and live, skim milk. —*Henry Ward Beecher (1813–1887)*

Life is an exciting business and most exciting when it is lived for others. —*Helen Keller (1880–1968)*

Life is either a daring adventure, or nothing. —*Helen Keller (1880–1968)*

We cannot live only for ourselves. A thousand fibers connect us with our fellow-men; and along these fibers, as sympathetic threads, our actions run as causes, and they come back to us as effects.
—*Herman Melville (1819–1891)*

One's most ordinary everyday mode of consciousness is being busy and lively and unconcerned with self.
—*Iris Murdoch (1919-)*

To be caught up in the nickel-dime, day-to-day, mundane affairs of everyday life is to lose sight of what life is intended to be. —*J. A. Kurtnacker, Jr. (1951-)*

The community you live in isn't an entity separate from your life. It's a representation of your life. You're the individual unit, the multiple of which is us. —*Jennifer James (1943-)*

But whosoever drinketh of the water that I shall give him shall never thirst; but the water that I shall give him shall be in him a well of water springing up into everlasting life. —*John 4:14*

The people of hope are those who believe that God created them for a purpose and that He will provide for their needs as they seek to fulfill His purpose in their lives. —*Pope John Paul II (1920-)*

You don't get to choose how you're going to die, or when. You can only decide how you're going to live. Now! —*Joan Baez (1941-)*

Growth is the only evidence of life. —*John Henry Newman (1801–1890)*

Life is easier to take than you'd think. All that is necessary is to accept the impossible, do without the indispensable, and bear the intolerable. —*Kathleen Norris (1880–1960)*

The central purpose of each life should be to dilute the misery in the world.
—*Karl Menninger (1893–1990)*

The sweetness of life lies in usefulness, like honey deep in the heart of a clover bloom.
—*Laura Ingalls Wilder (1867–1957)*

Every time you acquire a new interest, even more, a new accomplishment, you increase your power of life.
—*William Lyon Phelps (1865–1943)*

If a man has done nothing for a cause worth dying for, then he is not fit to live.
—*Martin Luther King, Jr. (1929–1968)*

If you want your life to be meaningful, go out and do something about it. —*Mary Louise Wiley (1958-)*

Life is not in having and getting, but in being and becoming. —*Matthew Arnold (1822–1888)*

Let us endeavor to live that when we come to die even the undertaker will be sorry.
—*Mark Twain (1835–1910)*

A good man doubles the length of his existence; to have lived so as to look back with pleasure on our past life is to live twice. —*Martial (40–103)*

Give life meaning through your commitments. —*Paul Reinert (1910-)*

I would have you learn this great fact: That a life of doing right is the wisest life there is.
—*Proverbs 4:11 (LB)*

For none of us lives to himself alone and none of us dies to himself alone. —*Romans 14:7 (NIV)*

The noblest contribution which one can make for the benefit of posterity is a good character; the richest bequest which any can leave is a shining, spotless example. —*Robert Charles Winthrop (1809–1894)*

If someone is wiser, if someone is happier by my having lived, my life will not have been in vain.
—*Roger Barnes (1897–1982)*

Not life, but a good life, is to be chiefly valued. —*Socrates (470–399 B.C.)*

Remember that you have only one soul; that you have only one death to die; that you have only one life, which is short and has to be lived by you alone; and there is only one glory, which is eternal. If you do this, there will be many things about which you care nothing. —*Teresa of Avila (1515–1582)*

Be all you can be and live a good life—have fun with it. —*Tina Yothers (1973-)*

Life offers no obstacles, only challenges! —*Unknown*

May your life be like the snowflake; leave a mark but not a stain. —*Unknown*

Old years and new years with all their pain and strife,
are but the bricks and steel and stone with which we fashion life. —*Unknown*

The game of life is a game of boomerangs. Our thoughts, deeds, and words return to us sooner or later with astounding accuracy. —*Unknown*

The value of life is measured not by its devotion but by its donation. —*Unknown*

Execute every act of thy life as though it were your last. —*Unknown*

It is good to have an end to journey toward; but it is the journey that matters, in the end.
—*Ursula K. le Guin (1929-)*

Life is a flower of which love is the honey. —*Victor Hugo (1802–1885)*

As we advance in life it becomes more and more difficult, but in fighting the difficulties the inmost strength of the heart is developed. —*Vincent van Gogh (1853–1890)*

Those who devote their lives to a cause greater than themselves always find a larger, fuller life than the one they surrendered. —*Wilbert E. Scheer (1909-)*

The best use of life is to invest it in something which will outlast life. —*William James (1842–1910)*

We are here to add what we can to, not to get what we can from, life. —*William Osler (1849–1919)*

To her fair works did Nature link,
The human soul that through me ran;
And much it grieved my heart to think,
What Man has made of Man.
—*William Wordsworth (1770–1850)*

LOVE

Compassion • Heart • Caring
Kindness • Feeling

Let us love others and let God make them good. —*A. Marilyn Bass (1938-)*

I bring to this great work a heart filled with love for my country and an honest desire to do what is right.
—*Abraham Lincoln (1809–1865)*

Beauty is in the heart of the beholder. —*Al Bernstein (1911–1987)*

The essence of love is found in man's inherent connection with God, manifested and strengthened by our willingness to give, or dulled and destroyed by our refusal to do so. —*Alan Calhoun (1957-)*

There isn't any formula or method. You learn to love by loving. . . . —*Aldous Huxley (1894–1963)*

To love for the sake of being loved is human, but to love for the sake of loving is angelic.
—*Alphonse de Lamartine (1790–1869)*

There is no harvest for the heart alone; The seed of love must be eternally resown.
—*Anne Morrow Lindbergh (1906-)*

Love is a force. . . . It is not a result; it is a cause. It is not a product; it produces.
—*Anne Morrow Lindbergh (1906-)*

Love is a power, like money, or steam or electricity. It is valueless unless you can give something else by means of it. —*Anne Morrow Lindbergh (1906-)*

To love deeply in one direction makes us more loving in all others. —*Anne Swetchine (1782–1857)*

Love does not consist in gazing at each other, but in looking together in the same direction.
—*Antoine de Saint-Exupery (1900–1944)*

Love life and life will love you back. Love people and they will love you back.
—*Arthur Rubinstein (1887–1982)*

The measure of a man's humanity is the extent and intensity of his love for mankind.
—*Ashley Montagu (1905-)*

Indiscriminate love for one's fellow-men is the highest virtue. . . . —*Ayn Rand (1905–1982)*

We are all born for love; it is the principle of existence and its only end.
—*Benjamin Disraeli (1804–1881)*

Great beauty, great strength, and great riches are really and truly of no great use; a right heart exceeds all.
—*Benjamin Franklin (1706–1790)*

Charity is that virtue by which part of that sincere love we have for ourselves is transferred pure and unmixed to others. —*Bernard Mandeville (1670–1733)*

The heart has its reason which reason does not know. —*Blaise Pascal (1623–1662)*

The man who foolishly does me wrong, I will return to him the protection of my most ungrudging love; and the more evil comes from him, the more good shall go from me. —*Buddha (556-480 B.C.)*

Love is patient, love is kind. It does not envy, it does not boast, it is not proud. —*I Corinthians 13:4 (NIV)*

There is nothing love cannot face; there is no limit to its faith, its hope, and its endurance.
—*I Corinthians 13:7 (NEB)*

Love never fails. —*I Corinthians 13:7 (NIV)*

Let love be your greatest aim. —*I Corinthians 14:1 (LB)*

Let all that you do be done in love. —*I Corinthians 16:14 (RSV)*

Knowledge puffeth up, but love builds up. —*I Corinthians 8:1 (RSV)*

Whoever loves his brother lives in the light. —*I John 2:10 (NIV)*

I glory in this world of men and women, torn with troubles, yet living on to love and laugh through it all. —*Carl Sandburg (1878–1967)*

Should any feeling but love and infinite compassion fill our hearts for all who live? —*Carmen Sylva (1843–1916)*

There is abundant testimony that if we choose love rather than self, we gain immeasurably. —*Charles Field (1836–1912)*

Carve your names on hearts and not on marble. —*Charles H. Spurgeon (1834–1892)*

The love of mother and child is beautiful; but there is a higher law than that—the love of one another. —*Charlotte Perkins Gilman (1860–1935)*

Love grows by service. —*Charlotte Perkins Gilman (1860–1935)*

He who is narrow of vision cannot be big of heart. —*Chinese Proverb*

And beyond all these things, put on love, which is the perfect bond of unity. —*Colossians 3:14 (NASV)*

True love is the surest foundation for peace. —*Corra May White Harris (1869–1935)*

Love is not only something you feel. It's something you do. —*David Wilkerson (1931-)*

Where the heart is willing it will find a thousand ways, but where it is unwilling it will find a thousand excuses. —*Dayak Proverb (Borneo)*

Love that asketh love again,
Finds the barter naught but pain;
Love that giveth in full store
Aye receives as much and more.
—*Dinah Mulock Craik (1826–1887)*

Trouble is a part of your life, and if you don't share it, you don't give the person who loves you enough chance to love you. —*Dinah Shore (1917-)*

It is always a feast where love is, and where love is, God is. —*Dorothy Day (1897–1980)*

We certainly can try to grow in love, and it is good practice, this giving what we've got, whether it is a cup of coffee or money to pay the grocery bill. —*Dorothy Day (1897–1980)*

We must lay one brick at a time, take one step at a time; we can be responsible only for the one action of the present moment. But we can beg for an increase of love in our hearts that will vitalize and transform all our individual actions. . . . —*Dorothy Day (1897–1980)*

Love is like quicksilver in the hand. Leave the fingers open, and it stays. Clutch it, and it darts away. —*Dorothy Parker (1893–1967)*

All for love, and nothing for reward. —*Edmund Spenser (1552–1599)*

Love grows by giving. The love we give away is the only love we keep. The only way to retain love is to give it away—art and religion the same. —*Elbert Hubbard (1856–1915)*

A mature person is one who has learned that there is both good and bad in all people and in all things, and who . . . deals charitably with the circumstances of life, knowing that . . . all of us need both love and charity. —*Eleanor Roosevelt (1884–1962)*

The ultimate lesson all of us have to learn is unconditional love, which includes not only others but ourselves as well. —*Elisabeth Kubler-Ross (1926-)*

We are made loveless by our possessions. —*Elizabeth of Thuringia (1206–1231)*

Love lights more fires than hate extinguishes. —*Ella Wheeler Wilcox (1855–1919)*

A weed is but an unloved flower. —*Ella Wheeler Wilcox (1855–1919)*

May you have warmth in your igloo, oil in your lamp, and peace in your heart. —*Eskimo Proverb*

I will give them an undivided heart and put a new spirit in them; I will remove their heart of stone and give them a heart of flesh. —*Ezekiel 11:19 (NIV)*

What is faith? What you do not see. What is hope? A great thing. What is charity? A great rarity. —*Facetiae Cantabrigiensis*

America has a willingness of heart. —*Francis Scott Key (1779–1843)*

The basic formula of all sin is: frustrated or neglected love. —*Franz Werfel (1890–1945)*

What! No star, and you are going out to sea? Marching, and you have no music? Traveling, and you have no book? What! No love, and you are going out to live? —*French Proverb*

It is not the brains that matter most, but that which guides them—character, the heart, generous qualities, progressive ideas. —*Feodor Dostoevski (1821–1881)*

You have been given freedom . . . to love and serve each other. —*Galatians 5:13 (LB)*

Love others as you love yourself. —*Galatians 5:14 (LB)*

If you really love something, set it free. If it comes back to you, it was meant to be. —*Gale Clarke (1949-)*

What is love? Love is when you care more about someone else than you care about yourself. —*George Akers (1926-)*

But is it what we love, or how we love, that makes true good? —*George Eliot (1819–1880)*

There is only one happiness in life, to love and be loved. —*George Sand (1804–1876)*

Almighty God, we make our earnest prayer. . . that Thou wilt incline the hearts of the citizens . . . to entertain a brotherly affection and love for one another and for their fellow citizens of the United States at large. —*George Washington (1732–1799)*

Love is a symbol of eternity. It wipes out all sense of time, destroying all memory of a beginning and all fear of an end. —*Germaine de Stael (1766–1817)*

To love is to place our happiness in the happiness of another. —*Gottfried von Liebnitz (1646–1716)*

Love was not given the human heart for careless dealing;
Its spark was lit that man might know Divine revealing.
—*Grace Goodhue Coolidge (1879–1957)*

Love never reasons, but profusely gives. —*Hannah Moore (1745–1833)*

Man can see his reflection in water only when he bends down close to it; and the heart of man, too, must lean down to the heart of his fellow; then it will see itself within his heart. —*Hasidic Proverb*

Let us consider how we may spur one another on toward love and good deeds. —*Hebrews 10:24 (NIV)*

Continue to love each other with true brotherly love. Don't forget to be kind to strangers, for some who have done this have entertained angels without realizing it! —*Hebrews 13:1,2 (LB)*

And the story of love is not important—what is important is that one is capable of love. It is perhaps the only glimpse we are permitted of eternity. —*Helen Hayes (1900-)*

A mother's love is fashioned after God's enduring love. It is endless and unfailing like the love of Him above. —*Helen Steiner Rice (1900–1981)*

Tell me how much you know of the sufferings of your fellow men and I will tell you how much you have loved them. —*Helmut Thielicke (1908–1986)*

Love is its own reward. —*Helmut Thielicke (1908–1986)*

There is no remedy for love but to love more. —*Henry David Thoreau (1817–1862)*

You will find, as you look back upon your life, that the moments that stand out, the moments when you have really lived, are the moments when you have done things in a spirit of love.
—*Henry Drummond (1854–1907)*

The only thing we can never get enough of is love. And the only thing we never give enough of is love.
—*Henry Miller (1891–1980)*

Time is too slow for those who wait, too swift for those who fear, too long for those who grieve, too short for those who rejoice, but for those who love; time is eternity. —*Henry Van Dyke (1852–1933)*

If we could read the secret history of our enemies, we should find in each one's life sorrow and suffering enough to disarm all hostility. —*Henry Wadsworth Longfellow (1807–1882)*

We should so live and labor in our times that what came to us as seed may go to the next generation as blossom, and what came to us as blossom may go to them as fruit. This expresses the true spirit in the love of mankind. —*Henry Ward Beecher (1813–1887)*

It is only important to love the world . . . to regard the world and ourselves and all beings with love, admiration and respect. —*Hermann Hesse (1877–1962)*

Love is to the moral nature what the sun is to the earth. —*Honore de Balzac (1799–1850)*

Let us not love in word, neither in tongue; but in deed and in truth. —*I John 3:18*

Our love must not be a thing of words and fine talk; it must be a thing of action and sincerity.
—*I John 3:18 (Barclay)*

If we love one another, God lives in us and His love is made complete in us. —*I John 4:12 (NIV)*

There is no fear in love; but perfect love casteth out fear. —*I John 4:18*

If anyone says, "I love God" yet hates his brother, he is a liar. —*I John 4:20 (NIV)*

Beloved, let us love one another . . . for God is love. —*I John 4:7-8*

There is no force more potent than love. —*Igor Stravinsky (1882–1971)*

We can only know love by loving. —*Iris Murdoch (1919-)*

All that is necessary to make this world a better place to live in is to love.
—*Isadora Duncan (1878–1927)*

So long as little children are allowed to suffer, there is no true love in this world.
—*Isadora Duncan (1878–1927)*

Goodness is love in action, love with its hand to the plow, love with the burden on its back, love following his footsteps who went about continually doing good. —*James Hamilton (1814–1867)*

Love is what you've been through with somebody. —*James Thurber (1894–1961)*

Little privations are easily endured when the heart is better treated than the body.
—*Jean-Jacques Rousseau (1712–1778)*

Age does not protect you from love, but love, to some extent, protects you from age.
—*Jeanne Moreau (1929)*

The heart sees better than the eye. —*Jewish Proverb*

Love one human being purely and warmly, and you will love all. The heart in this heaven, like the sun in its course, sees nothing from the dew drop to the ocean, but a mirror which it brightens, and warms and fills. —*Johann Richter (1763–1825)*

It is not flesh and blood but the heart which makes us fathers and sons.
—*Johann von Schiller (1759–1805)*

Love of truth shows itself in this, that a man knows how to find and value the good in everything.
—*Johann Wolfgang von Goethe (1749–1832)*

A man doesn't learn to understand anything unless he loves it.
—*Johann Wolfgang von Goethe (1749–1832)*

A new commandment I give unto you, that ye love one another. —*John 13:34*

Greater love hath no man than this, that a man lay down his life for his friends. —*John 15:13*

This is my command: Love each other. —*John 15:17 (NIV)*

In prayer it is better to have a heart without words than words without a heart.
—*John Bunyan (1628–1688)*

I believe that love is the greatest thing in the world, that it alone can overcome hate and that right can and will triumph over might. —*John D. Rockefeller (1839–1937)*

I know not where His islands lift
Their fronded palms in air,
I only know I cannot drift
Beyond His love and care.
—*John Greenleaf Whittier (1807–1892)*

Where you find no love, put love and you will find love. —*John of the Cross (1542–1591)*

Love supposes, is, and does many things, but basically it is practiced in the act of sharing.
—*John Powell (1925-)*

The only truly happy people are those who have found someone or some cause to love and belong to.
—*John Powell (1925-)*

The question is not so much what the hand is doing (passing over some cash or a check) but what the heart is thinking while the hand is doing it. —*John R. W. Stott (1921-)*

When love and skill work together, expect a masterpiece. —*John Ruskin (1819–1900)*

Life is a magic vase filled to the brim, so made that you cannot dip from it nor draw from it; but it overflows into the hand that drops treasures into it. Drop in malice and it overflows hate; drop in charity and it overflows love. —*John Ruskin (1819–1900)*

So far as true love influences our minds, so far we feel a desire to make use of every opportunity to lessen the distresses of the afflicted, and to increase the happiness of the creation . . . to turn all the treasures we possess into the channel of universal love becomes the business of our lives.
—*John Woolman (1720–1772)*

In all people there are two sets of feelings: One is fear, the other is love. If there is fear, then we shrink as a person. But love, wow! That can move mountains! —*Jorgen Roed (1936-)*

Love exalts as much as glory does. —*Juliette Drouet (1806–1883)*

From the beginning of life to its end, love is the only emotion which matters. —*June Callwood (1924-)*

Life without love is like a tree without blossom and fruit. —*Kahlil Gibran (1883–1931)*

Our lives are shaped by those who love us as well as those who refuse to love us.
—*Karl Menninger (1893–1990)*

Love cures people—both the ones who give it and the ones who receive it.
—*Karl Menninger (1893–1990)*

Allah . . . gave you ears and eyes and hearts, so that you may give thanks. —*Koran, Sura XVI.80*

By the accident of fortune a man may rule the world for a time, but by virtue of love he may rule the world forever. —*Lao-tzu (604–531 B.C.)*

Nothing cures like time and love. —*Laura Nyro (1947-)*

When man has love he is no longer at the mercy of forces greater than himself, for he, himself, becomes the powerful force. —*Leo Buscaglia (1925-)*

Choose the way of life. Choose the way of love. Choose the way of caring. Choose the way of goodness. It's up to you. It's your choice. —*Leo Buscaglia (1925-)*

I have a very strong feeling that the opposite of love is not hate—it's apathy. —*Leo Buscaglia (1925-)*

A life lived in love will never be dull. —*Leo Buscaglia (1925-)*

A life without love, no matter how many other things we have, is an empty meaningless one.
—*Leo Buscaglia (1925-)*

A loving person recognizes needs. —*Leo Buscaglia (1925-)*

Real love always creates, it never destroys. In this lies man's only promise. —*Leo Buscaglia (1925-)*

Love acquires meaning only as it's shared. —*Leo Buscaglia (1925-)*

I believe that the reason of life is for each of us simply to grow in love. —*Leo Tolstoy (1828–1910)*

You shall love your neighbor as yourself. —*Leviticus 19:18 (RSV)*

Love is the foundation and keystone of life. —*Lou Austin (1891-)*

Love that is hoarded moulds at last
Until we know some day
The only thing we ever have
Is what we give away.
—*Louis Ginsberg (1896–1976)*

Love is the only thing that we can carry with us when we go, and it makes the end so easy.
—*Louisa May Alcott (1832–1888)*

Love is a great beautifier. —*Louisa May Alcott (1832–1888)*

Wherever there is a human being, there is an opportunity for kindness.
—*Lucius Annaeus Seneca (4 B.C.–A.D. 65)*

If you love only those who love you . . . if you help only those who help you . . . what merit is that to you?
—*Luke 6:32,33 (Moffatt)*

But love your enemies, do good, and lend, hoping for nothing in return; and your reward will be great, and you will be sons of the Most High. —*Luke 6:35 (RSV)*

From all that fate has brought to me,
I strive to learn humility,
And trust in Him who rules above,
Whose universal law is love.
—*Lydia Maria Child (1802–1880)*

Love conquers all except poverty and a toothache. —*Mae West (1892–1980)*

Peace between countries must rest on the solid foundation of love between individuals.
—*Mahatma Gandhi (1869–1948)*

My life is an indivisible whole, and all my activities run into one another; and they all have their rise in my insatiable love of mankind. —*Mahatma Gandhi (1869–1948)*

Love has more force than a besieging army. —*Mahatma Gandhi (1869–1948)*

People who matter are most aware that everyone else does, too. —*Malcolm S. Forbes (1919–1990)*

Ever since our love for machines replaced the love we used to have for our fellow man, catastrophes proceeded to increase. —*Man Ray (1890–1976)*

Without love, all the merits and power of man are nothing. —*Margaret of Navarre (1492–1549)*

The human heart, at whatever age, opens only to the heart that opens in return. —*Maria Edgeworth (1767–1849)*

Love is not getting but giving. —*Marie Dressler (1873–1934)*

Praise is well, compliment is well, but affection—that is the last and most precious reward that any man can win, whether by character or achievement. —*Mark Twain (1835–1910)*

Some people, no matter how old they get, never lose their beauty—they merely move it from their faces into their hearts —*Martin Buxbaum (1912–1991)*

Faith, like light, should always be simple and unbending; while love, like warmth, should beam forth on every side, and bend to every necessity of our brethren. —*Martin Luther (1483–1546)*

Love is the only force capable of transforming an enemy into a friend. —*Martin Luther King, Jr. (1929–1968)*

I want you to say that I tried to love and serve humanity. I won't have the fine and luxurious things of life to leave behind. But I just want a committed life to leave behind. —*Martin Luther King, Jr. (1929–1968)*

What can pay love but love? —*Mary de la Riveire Manley (1663–1724)*

Love is . . . the lamp that lights the universe: without that light . . . the earth is a barren promontory and man the quintessence of dust. —*Mary Elizabeth Braddon (1837–1915)*

Love your neighbor as yourself. —*Matthew–19:19 (NIV)*

It is sad not to be loved, but it is much sadder not to be able to love. —*Miguel de Unamuno (1864–1936)*

Blessed are the well-loved; they exude a strength and a joy that others try to struggle through life without. —*Millie Thornton (1958-)*

To live without loving is not really to live. —*Molière (1622–1673)*

Take love away from life and you take away its pleasures. —*Molière (1622–1673)*

Love the beautiful, seek out the true. Wish for the good, and the best do.
—*Moses Mendelssohn (1729–1786)*

Even the rich are hungry for love, for being cared for, for being wanted, for having someone to call their own. —*Mother Teresa (1910-)*

Small things, done in great love, bring joy and peace. —*Mother Teresa (1910-)*

If you judge people, you have no time to love them. —*Mother Teresa (1910-)*

Love is a fruit in season at all times, and within the reach of every hand. —*Mother Teresa (1910-)*

Every creative act of ours in relation to other people—an act of love, of pity, of help, of peacemaking—not merely has a future but is eternal. —*Nikolay Berdyayev (1874–1948)*

Scatter good will and love and prayers all around, everywhere, and you will be astonished, not only by what it does for other people, but how it comes back to you in generous abundance.
—*Norman Vincent Peale (1898–1993)*

If your life has been enriched by love, once or more than once . . . the memory of it . . . never leaves you.
—*Olivia De Havilland (1916-)*

A bell is not a bell until you ring it.
A song is not a song until you sing it.
Love in your heart is not put there to stay.
Love is not love until you give it way.
—*Oscar Hammerstein (1895–1960)*

Keep love in your heart. A life without it is like a sunless garden when the flowers are dead. The consciousness of loving and being loved brings a warmth and richness to life that nothing else can bring.
—*Oscar Wilde (1854–1900)*

You must be one in your attitude to life and one in your sympathy with each other. Love must be the hall-mark of your society. You must be deeply concerned for others. —*I Peter 3:8 (B)*

Most important of all, continue to show deep love for each other, for love makes up for many of your faults.
—*I Peter 4:8 (LB)*

A man without ambition is dead. A man with ambition but no love is dead. A man with ambition and love for his blessings here on earth is ever so alive. —*Pearl Bailey (1918–1990)*

To love is to know the sacrifices which eternity exacts from life. —*Pearl Craigie (1867–1906)*

On this earth, though far and near, without love, there's only fear. —*Pearl S. Buck (1892–1973)*

True love in this differs from gold and clay,
That to divide is not to take away.
—*Percy Bysshe Shelley (1792–1822)*

I think true love is never blind,
But rather brings an added light,
An inner vision quick to find
The beauties hid from common sight.
—*Phoebe Cary (1824–1874)*

The worst prison would be a closed heart. —*Pope John Paul II (1920-)*

Peace must be realized in truth; it must be built upon justice; it must be animated in love; it must be brought to being in freedom. —*Pope John XXIII (1881–1963)*

Love can neither be bought nor sold; its only price being love. —*Proverb*

In love is no lack. —*Proverb*

Let my love like sunlight surround you, yet give you illumined freedom.
—*Rabindranath Tagore (1861–1941)*

We live in this world when we love it. —*Rabindranath Tagore (1861–1941)*

He who wants to do good knocks at the gate; he who loves finds the gate open.
—*Rabindranath Tagore (1861–1941)*

For one human being to love another: that is perhaps the most difficult of all our tasks.
—*Rainer Maria Rilke (1875–1926)*

Love consists in this, that two solitudes protect and touch and greet each other.
—*Rainer Maria Rilke (1875–1926)*

Love, you know, seeks to make happy rather than to be happy. —*Ralph Connor (1860–1937)*

He who loves not, lives not. —*Ramon Lull (1232–1316)*

Love without laughter can be grim and oppressive. Laughter without love can be derisive and venomous. Together they make for greatness of spirit. —*Robert K. Greenleaf (1904-1990)*

Love is the only bow on life's dark cloud. —*Robert G. Ingersoll (1833-1899)*

Love is indestructible;
Its holy flame forever burneth;
From heaven it came,
To heaven returneth.
—*Robert Southey (1744-1843)*

Love is everybody's business. —*Rod McKuen (1933-)*

The mystery of God is enfleshed in unexpected people in unexpected places. Our task: to be open to the mystery—and enflesh it in love. —*Roger L. Robbennolt (1934-)*

I should like to feel that the hearts of those who help the poor are warmed toward them. . . .
—*Rose Hawthorne Lathrop (1851-1926)*

Love brings light into the world. —*Jalal-Ud-Din Rumi (1207-1273)*

Man looks at the outward appearance, but the Lord looks at the heart. —*I Samuel 16:7 (NIV)*

Many waters cannot quench love, neither can floods drown it. If a man offered for love all the wealth of his house, it would be utterly scorned. —*Song of Solomon 8:7 (RSV)*

What does love look like? It has the hands to help others. It has the feet to hasten to the poor and needy. It has the eyes to see misery and want. It has the ears to hear the sighs and sorrows of men. That is what love looks like. —*St. Augustine (354-430)*

Human nature has grounds for hope, because love, in a sense, is inexhaustible. —*Steve Allen (1921-)*

Love that is not expressed in loving action does not really exist. —*Sydney J. Harris (1917-)*

Accustom yourself continually to make many acts of love, for they enkindle and melt the soul.
—*Teresa of Avila (1515-1582)*

We give from the head and the heart. —*The Meadows Foundation of Dallas*

Love one another in deed, and in word, and in the inclination of the soul.
—*The Twelve Testaments - Gad*

Whoever loves much, does much. —*Thomas a'Kempis (1380–1471)*

He who loves with purity considers not the gift of the lover, but the love of a giver.
—*Thomas a'Kempis (1380–1471)*

To live in hearts we leave behind is not to die. —*Thomas Campbell (1777–1844)*

The wealth of a man is the number of things which he loves and blesses, which he is loved and blessed by.
—*Thomas Carlyle (1795–1881)*

He that plants trees loves others besides himself. —*Thomas Fuller (1654–1734)*

The heart that has truly loved never forgets, but, as truly, loves on to the close.
—*Thomas Moore (1779–1852)*

There is a land of the living and of the dead, and the bridge is love, the only survival, the only meaning.
—*Thornton Wilder (1897–1975)*

It's in our self-interest to help one another. The important thing is to give of yourself.
—*Timothy Shriver (1959-)*

Love is the doorway through which the human soul passes from selfishness to service and from solitude to kinship with all mankind. —*Unknown*

Love is the one commodity that multiplies when you give it away. . . . Not only is it the sweet mystery of life, it is the most powerful motivation known to man. —*Unknown*

Love will find a way. Indifference will find an excuse. —*Unknown*

Man's greatest need is to be loved and, in turn, to love others. —*Unknown*

The thought of the love of God cannot be grasped in the slightest degree even as a working hypothesis, by a man who does not know human love. —*Unknown*

The cure for all the ills and wrongs, the cares, the sorrows, and the crime of humanity, all lie in that one word "love." —*Unknown*

Mind your heart. Don't let anything but good get into your heart—to think good, to do good, to love good.
—*Unknown*

The value of the gift is in the love of the giver. —*Unknown*

The hater is a fool who does not know that to love is the greatest of luxuries. —*Unknown*

Mother weaves her loving art and leaves her magic in our hearts. —*Unknown*

If ever a man shall live who has infinite power, he will be found to be one who has infinite love. —*Unknown*

You cannot love much and give little. How much you love can be measured by how much you give. —*Unknown*

Learn from nature the profusion of her gifts. As you daily realize more and more the generosity of the Divine Giver, learn increasingly to give. Love grows by giving. You cannot give bountifully without being filled with a sense of giving yourself with the gift, and you cannot so give without love passing from you to the one who receives. —*Unknown*

Every activity of man should add to the intangible values of life as well as to the tangible. —*Unknown*

Sentimentality comes easy. But caring is hard—it involves doing. —*Unknown*

The love you give away is the only love you can keep and carry in your heart. —*Unknown*

If we carry any possession from this world, it is the memory of a great love. —*Unknown*

Life is sometimes hard to love, though we must love it because we have no other. To fail to love it is to cease to exist. —*Unknown*

Live simply; love extravagantly. —*Unknown*

Help me to live time, not just to use it; to breathe it in, and return it in acts of love and presence. —*Unknown*

Love does not die easily. It is a living thing. It thrives in the face of all life's hazards, save one—neglect. —*Unknown*

Those who see the needs of the world—the helpless children, the hungry children, the unclothed children, the unhealed children, the uneducated children, the unloved children of every age—these will find God. —*Unknown*

Love is a little word; people make it big. —*Unknown*

Love is a priceless commodity. It's the only thing you can give away and still keep. —*Unknown*

Love is a short word but it contains everything. —*Unknown*

Take time to love and be loved. It is the privilege of the gods. —*Unknown*

Love doesn't just sit there, like a stone, it has to be made, like bread; remade all the time, made new.
—*Ursula K. le Guin (1929-)*

The best way to know God is to love many things. —*Vincent van Gogh (1853–1890)*

Love is never lost. If not reciprocated, it will flow back and soften and purify the heart.
—*Washington Irving (1783–1859)*

In every pardon there is love. —*Welsh Proverb*

What better way is there to make men love one another than to make men understand one another? True charity comes only with clarity—just as "mercy" is but justice that understands. Surely the root of all evil is the inability to see clearly that which is. —*William Durant (1861–1947)*

The love of liberty is the love of others; the love of power is the love of ourselves.
—*William Hazlitt (1778–1830)*

Love sought is good, but given unsought is better. —*William Shakespeare (1564–1616)*

Who can sever love from charity? —*William Shakespeare (1564–1616)*

I don't want to live—I want to love first, and live incidentally. —*Zelda Sayre Fitzgerald (1900–1948)*

Nobody has ever measured . . . how much the heart can hold. —*Zelda Sayre Fitzgerald (1900–1948)*

Loving, like prayer, is a power as well as a process. It's curative. It is creative. —*Zona Gale (1874–1938)*

Love is like the sea, it's a moving thing; but still it takes its shape from the shore it meets and it's different with every shore. —*Zora Neale Hurston (1903–1960)*

Know well that a hundred holy temples of wood and stone have not the value of one understanding heart.
—*Zoroastrian Scriptures*

PATRIOTISM

Freedom • Liberty • Democracy
America • Rights

Freedom is not constituted primarily of privileges but of responsibilities. —*Albert Camus (1913–1960)*

Freedom cannot be given; it must be purchased. —*Booker T. Washington (1856–1915)*

The benefit of one is the benefit of all, and the neglect of one is the neglect of all.
—*Calvin Coolidge (1872–1933)*

True freedom has always moved forward in the hearts and upon the shoulders of willing volunteers.
—*Chet Damron (1934-)*

If a man does only what is required of him, he is a slave. If a man does more than is required of him, he is a free man. —*Chinese Proverb*

Memorial Day is one of the most significant and beautiful occasions of the year. It shows the sentiment of the people toward those who gave their lives for a good cause and it teaches a lesson in patriotism which is without parallel. —*C. E. Allison (1847–1908)*

On discovering America: It is the most beautiful land that human eyes have seen. There is no better land or people. They love their neighbors as they do themselves, and their speech is the world's softest, tame, and always with a smile. —*Christopher Columbus (1451–1506)*

God grants liberty only to those who love it, and are always ready to guard and defend it.
—*Daniel Webster (1782–1852)*

Freedom is not worth fighting for if it means no more than license for everyone to get as much as he can for himself. —*Dorothy Canfield Fisher (1879–1958)*

The true slogan of a true democracy is not 'Let the Government do it' but rather, 'Let's do it ourselves' . . . This is the spirit of a people dedicated to helping themselves—and one another.
—*Dwight D. Eisenhower (1890–1969)*

To have built oneself into the structure of undying institutions, to have aided in the development of these priceless instruments of civilization, is to have lived, not in vain, but to have lived in perpetuity.
—*Elihu Root (1845–1937)*

Every American takes pride in our tradition of hospitality to men of all races and creeds. We must be constantly vigilant against the attacks of intolerance and injustice. We must scrupulously guard the civil rights and civil liberties of all citizens, whatever their background. We must remember that any oppression, any injustice, any hatred, is a wedge designed to attack civilization.
—*Franklin D. Roosevelt (1882–1945)*

The life of a nation is secure only while the nation is honest, truthful, and virtuous.
—*Frederick Douglass (1817–1895)*

He who has lost his freedom has nothing else to lose. —*German Proverb*

There were two things I had a right to, liberty and death. If I cannot have one, I would have the other.
—*Harriet Tubman (1823–1913)*

But what is Freedom? Rightly understood,
A universal license to be good.
—*Hartley Coleridge (1796–1849)*

Who ever walked behind anyone to freedom? If we can't go hand in hand, I don't want to go.
—*Hazel Scott (1920-)*

The essence of American liberty is to assure men the secured right to every activity which does not trespass the rights of others. —*Herbert C. Hoover (1874–1964)*

The hope of America and the world is to regenerate liberty with its responsibilities and its obligations—not to abandon it. —*Herbert C. Hoover (1874–1964)*

Liberty is not to be had or held without effort. —*Herbert C. Hoover (1874–1964)*

America did not invent human rights. Human rights invented America. — *Jimmy Carter (1924-)*

America! America! God shed His grace on thee
And crown thy good with brotherhood
From sea to shining sea!
—*Katherine Lee Bates (1859–1929)*

Freedom never yet was given to nations as a gift, but only as a reward, bravely earned by one's own exertions. —*Lajos Kossuth (1802–1894)*

There is little hope for democracy if the hearts of men and women in democratic societies cannot be touched by a call to something greater than themselves. —*Margaret Thatcher (1925-)*

If Negro freedom is taken away, or that of any minority group, the freedom of all the people is taken away. —*Paul Robeson (1898–1976)*

One of the indispensable foods for the human soul is liberty. —*Simone Weil (1909–1943)*

What can be heavier in wealth than freedom? —*Sylvia Ashton-Warner (1908–1984)*

Those who expect to reap the blessing of freedom must undertake to support it. —*Thomas Paine (1737–1809)*

The function of freedom is to free somebody else. —*Toni Morrison (1931-)*

If a nation values anything more than freedom, it will lose its freedom, and the irony of it is that if it is comfort or money that it values more, it will lose that too. —*W. Somerset Maugham (1874–1965)*

The history of every country begins in the heart of a man or a woman. —*Willa Cather (1873–1947)*

The cost of liberty is less than the price of repression. —*William Edward Burghardt Du Bois (1868–1963)*

PHILANTHROPY
Community • Giving • Action
Involvement • Sincerity

Philanthropist: a rich (and usually bald) old gentleman who has trained himself to grin while his conscience is picking his pocket. —*Ambrose Bierce (1842–1914)*

Philanthropy is a ministry. — *Arthur C. Frantzreb (1920-)*

Successful philanthropy ought to be the by-product of good management.
— *Arthur C. Frantzreb (1920-)*

One of the greatest limitations in our world of philanthropy is the lack of understanding that there is, within each person, a yearning to be part of something larger than ourselves. Recognizing that need and meeting it is the reward of our ministry for humankind. — *Arthur C. Frantzreb (1920-)*

Philanthropy is not a geographic term. —*Charles D. Brooks (1930-)*

Philanthropy, like charity, must begin at home. —*Charles Lamb (1775–1834)*

Philanthropy is an expression of man's concern for man. —*Charles E. Bradford (1925-)*

A wise philanthropist, in a time of famine, would vote for nothing but a supply of toothpicks.
—*Douglas Jerrold (1803–1857)*

Philanthropy flows from a loving heart not an overstuffed pocketbook. —*Douglas M. Lawson (1936-)*

Philanthropy is the secret that unlocks the storehouse of life's blessings. —*Douglas M. Lawson (1936-)*

Philanthropy is the mystical mingling of a joyous giver, an artful asker, and a grateful recipient.
—*Douglas M. Lawson (1936-)*

The philanthropic experience is the healthiest way to live life fully. —*Douglas M. Lawson (1936-)*

Like happiness, philanthropy was born a twin. The giving that proceeds from a desire for personal credit or satisfaction may be tax-deductible, but it is scarcely philanthropy. —*F. Emerson Andrews (1902–1978)*

The most effective philanthropy helps people help themselves and preserves their self-respect. But government should not diminish its role in providing human services, since the financial impact of philanthropy is about one-tenth that of all levels of government. —*Eugene C. Dorsey (1927-)*

Do good through philanthropy, make money, have fun, all at the same time.
—*George M. Jaffin (1905-)*

Philanthropy, like Red Cross voluntarism, is realizing the enhancing influence of cultural diversity. Inviting the full participation of all the community's resources leads to win-win situations.
—*Gwen Jackson (1928-)*

The vineyards of philanthropy are pleasant places, and I would hope good men and women will be drawn there. . . . If these vineyards are to thrive and bear their best fruit, they must always have first-class attention. —*Harold J. Seymour (1894–1968)*

Philanthropy is almost the only virtue which is sufficiently appreciated by mankind.
—*Henry David Thoreau (1817–1862)*

Philanthropy is not a matter of the rich helping the non-rich, it's the community extending itself out to the community. —*J. Herman Blake (1934-)*

Philanthropy lies at the heart of human greatness. —*J. Patrick Ryan (1940-)*

The work of philanthropy has no parallel in this country in our day. And we must bring to this work a dedication, a love, an interest, an importance and an urgency which show through to every volunteer we enlist and every prospect we solicit. —*James W. Frick (1924-)*

When it comes to philanthropy, write a check your heart can cash. —*Jackie A. Strange (1927-)*

Inside every woman is a potential major philanthropist waiting to emerge. —*Joan M. Fisher (1947-)*

Philanthropy is the rent we pay for the joy and privilege we have for our space on this earth.
—*Jerold Panas (1928-)*

If charity cost nothing, the world would be full of philanthropists. —*Jewish Proverb*

The best philanthropy is a search for cause, an attempt to cure evils at their source.
—*John D. Rockefeller (1839–1937)*

You cannot hope to build a better world without improving the individuals. To that end each of us must work for his own improvement, and at the same time share a general responsibility for all humanity, our particular duty being to aid those to whom we think we can be most useful. —*Marie Curie (1867–1934)*

I have tried to keep things in my hands and lost them all, but what I have given into the Lord's hands I still possess. —*Martin Luther King, Jr. (1929–1968)*

Philanthropy is commendable, but it must not cause the philanthropist to overlook the circumstances of economic injustice which make philanthropy necessary. —*Martin Luther King, Jr. (1929–1968)*

Philanthropy is loving, ameliorative, *–1993* revolutionary; it wakens lofty desires, new possibilities, achievements, and energies; . . . it touches thought to spiritual issues, systematizes action, and ensures success. —*Mary Baker Eddy (1821–1910)*

Do we live for or do we live off philanthropy? —*Robert L. Payton (1926-)*

We cannot preserve philanthropic and charitable values if we detach them completely from our fundamental personal beliefs and convictions. —*Robert L. Payton (1926-)*

Philanthropy is the principal social institution that provides instruction in voluntary service.
—*Robert L. Payton (1926-)*

The philanthropic tradition . . . is older than democracy, older than Christianity, and older than higher education. It gives form and purpose to personal and social life that cannot be provided by the self-interest of economic enterprise or required by the mandate of political institutions. —*Robert L. Payton (1926-)*

Philanthropy is the duty of how we should behave when things go wrong for people, and how we can help to make things better for everyone—voluntarily, without being required to do it by the government, and for others, without private gain for ourselves. —*Robert L. Payton (1926-)*

We should never lose sight of the very close link between individual giving and the formation of philanthropic traditions. —*Robert L. Payton (1926-)*

Philanthropy requires thought, action, and passion. —*Robert L. Payton (1926-)*

People want their lives to have made a difference. Philanthropic giving is a means to that end.
—*Sheree Parris Nudd (1954-)*

Every philanthropic endeavor needs enough failures to keep it humble and enough victories to keep it succeeding. —*Solon B. Cousins (1925-)*

In times of great need we are all rich enough to be philanthropists. —*Unknown*

Philanthropists are people who give away what they could be getting back. —*Unknown*

The true worth of a man is to be measured by the objects he pursues. —*Unknown*

Definition of a philanthropist: A generous person despised by relatives. —*Unknown*

True charity consists of helping those you have every reason to believe would NOT help you. —*Unknown*

Philanthropy proves that though money is the root of all evil, it is also the route of much good. —*Unknown*

Money does not necessarily ruin a man: many millionaire philanthropists learned true charity only after acquiring their millions. —*Unknown*

Apart from the ballot box, philanthropy presents the one opportunity the individual has to express his meaningful choice over the direction in which any society will progress. —*Unknown*

The path of philanthropy is filled with toll stations. —*Unknown*

In philanthropy, benefactions speak louder than words. —*Unknown*

SERVICE

Help • Minister • Attend
Duty • Altruism

Let us have faith that right makes might; and in that faith let us to the end, dare to do our duty as we understand it. —*Abraham Lincoln (1809–1865)*

Try not to become a man of success but rather try to become a man of value.
—*Albert Einstein (1879–1955)*

I don't know what your destiny will be, but one thing I know: the only ones among you who will be really happy are those who have sought and found how to serve. —*Albert Schweitzer (1875–1965)*

If affirmation for life is genuine, it will demand from all that they should sacrifice a portion of their own lives for others. —*Albert Schweitzer (1875–1965)*

There is no higher religion than human service. To work for the common good is the greatest creed.
—*Albert Schweitzer (1875–1965)*

He who serves his brother best gets nearer God than all the rest. —*Alexander Pope (1688–1744)*

True worth is in being, not in seeming—
In doing, each day that goes by,
Some little good—not in dreaming
Of the great things to do by and by.
—*Alice Cary (1820–1871)*

Corporations must serve society, even seek out ways to do so. —*Andrew Heiskell (1915-)*

How lovely to think that no one need wait a moment: we can start now, start slowly changing the world! How lovely that everyone, great and small, can make a contribution toward introducing justice straightaway! —*Anne Frank (1929–1945)*

Whatever good there is in the world I inherit from the courage and work of those who went before me. I, in turn, have a responsibility to make things better for those who will inherit the earth from me.
—*Arthur Dobrin (1943-)*

He profits most who serves best. —*Arthur F. Sheldon (1868–1935)*

People who fight fire with fire usually end up with ashes. —*Abigail Van Buren (1918-)*

The relationship is the communication bridge between people. —*Alfred Kadushin (1916-)*

May we never be tempted to forget that there can be no real success apart from service, that success is but service visualized. —*B. C. Forbes (1880–1954)*

He who is ambitious to succeed must learn how he can best serve, how he can fit himself to earn high rewards, how, in short he can make himself useful beyond the ordinary. —*B. C. Forbes (1880–1954)*

To get the most out of the world one must conscientiously strive to put the most into it. Life without worthy ideals becomes wholly unsatisfying, sour. If our supreme objective is to serve, no blow fate may administer can daunt us. —*B. C. Forbes (1880–1954)*

The be-all and end-all of life should not be to get rich, but to enrich the world.
—*B. C. Forbes (1880–1954)*

Show me the businessman or institution not guided by sentiment and service, by the idea that "he profits most who serves best," and I will show you a man or an outfit that is dead or dying.
—*B. F. Harris (1921-)*

When men and governments work intelligently and far-sightedly for the good of others, they achieve their own prosperity, too. —*Barbara Ward (1914–1981)*

Every single ancient wisdom and religion will tell you the same thing: Don't live entirely for yourself; live for other people. Don't get stuck inside your own ego, because it will become a prison in no time flat. . . .
—*Barbara Ward (1914–1981)*

When I am employed in serving others, I do not look upon myself as conferring favors but paying debts.
—*Benjamin Franklin (1706–1790)*

I early found that when I worked for myself alone, others alone worked for me, but when I worked for others also, others also worked for me. —*Benjamin Franklin (1706–1790)*

Doing nothing for others is the undoing of ourselves. —*Benjamin Franklin (1706–1790)*

Serving God is doing good to man. But praying is thought an easier service and is therefore more generally chosen. —*Benjamin Franklin (1706–1790)*

The most acceptable service of God is doing good to man. —*Benjamin Franklin (1706–1790)*

A human being is happiest and most successful when dedicated to a cause outside his own individual, selfish satisfaction. —*Benjamin Spock (1903-)*

I challenge a new generation of young Americans to a season of service—to act on your idealism by helping troubled children, keeping company with those in need, reconnecting our torn communities. There is so much to be done—enough indeed for millions of others who are still young in spirit to give themselves in service too. —*Bill Clinton (1946-)*

This may be the day God gives me a great opportunity to serve someone who needs help from me. —*Bill Grosz (1937-)*

Along the way of our service to others and community, we learn that a very large side benefit is an enormous sense of personal satisfaction, personal purpose and personal worth. —*Brian O'Connell (1930-)*

No enterprise can exist for itself alone. It ministers to some great need, it performs some great service, not for itself, but for others. —*Calvin Coolidge (1872–1933)*

They serve God well, who serve his creatures. —*Caroline Sheridan Norton (1808–1877)*

Service to a just cause rewards the worker with more real happiness and satisfaction than any other venture of life. —*Carrie Chapman Catt (1859–1947)*

You have got to be a servant to somebody or something. —*Charles F. Kettering (1876–1958)*

I have indeed lived nominally fifty years, but deduct out of them the hours which I have lived to other people, and not to myself, and you will find me still a young fellow. For that is the only true time, which a man can properly call his own, that which he has all to himself; the rest, though in some sense he may be said to live it, is other people's time, not his. —*Charles Lamb (1775–1834)*

I have been the recipient of love and service, therefore I can love and serve. There is great satisfaction in service to others, in . . . seeing people and their conditions change. —*Clarence E. Hodges (1939-)*

I want to help people feel good about themselves, and in turn, about others, so they will have the desire to help others rather than being a selfish threat to society. —*Clarence E. Hodges (1939-)*

When you are laboring for others, let it be with the same zeal as if it were for yourself. —*Confucius (551–479 B.C.)*

You must not think of making the good you do a pouring of water into a pump to draw out something for yourselves. —*Cotton Mather (1663–1728)*

In our era, the road to holiness necessarily passes through the world of action. —*Dag Hammarskjold (1905–1961)*

A willing helper does not wait until he is asked. —*Danish Proverb*

Out of the best and most productive years of each man's life, he should carve a segment in which he puts his private career aside to serve his community and his country. —*David Lilienthal (1899–1981)*

The rare individual who unselfishly tries to serve others has an enormous advantage. He has little competition. —*Dale Carnegie (1888–1955)*

What we are in ourselves, and what we owe to others makes us a complete whole. —*Dietrich Bonhoeffer (1906–1945)*

To give real service you must add something which cannot be bought or measured with money, and that is sincerity and integrity. —*Donald A. Adams (1881–1971)*

Serving the needs of others is the light that brightens each day. —*Douglas M. Lawson (1936-)*

Our rewards in life will always be in direct ratio to our service. —*Earl Nightingale (1921-)*

The making of money, the accumulation of material power, is not all there is to living. . . and the man who misses this truth misses the greatest joy and satisfaction that can come into his life—service for others. —*Edward Bok (1863–1930)*

Every action of our lives touches on some chord that will vibrate in eternity. —*Edwin Hubbel Chapin (1814–1880)*

That is good which serves—man is the important item, this earth is the place, and the time is now. —*Elbert Hubbard (1856–1915)*

That which does not serve, dies. —*Elbert Hubbard (1856–1915)*

Take us on the quest of service,
Kingly servant of man's needs.
Let us work with Thee for others,
Anywhere Thy purpose leads.
—*Eleanor B. Stock (1900-)*

If I were asked what is the best thing one can expect in life, I would say—the privilege of being useful.
—*Eleanor Roosevelt (1884–1962)*

'Twas her thinking of others made you think of her. —*Elizabeth Barrett Browning (1806–1861)*

The sweetest lives are those to duty wed, whose deeds both great and small are close-knit strands of an unbroken thread, where love enables all. —*Elizabeth Barrett Browning (1806–1861)*

A poor man served by thee shall make thee rich; a sick man helped by thee shall make thee strong; thou shalt be served thyself by every sense of service which thou renderest.
—*Elizabeth Barrett Browning (1806–1861)*

With every deed you are sowing a seed,
Though the harvest you may not see.
—*Ella Wheeler Wilcox (1855–1919)*

The life that will be preserved is the life that is freely given in service to God and man.
—*Ellen G. White (1827–1915)*

I slept, and dreamed that life was beauty: I woke, and found that life was duty.
—*Ellen Sturgis Hooper (1816–1841)*

The way not to lead a monotonous life is to live for others. —*Fulton J. Sheen (1895–1979)*

Today, I ask all Americans and all institutions, large and small, to make service central to your life and work. —*George Bush (1924-)*

Together, we can show that what matters in the end are not possessions. What matters is engaging in the high moral principle of serving one another. That's the story of America that we can write through voluntary service. —*George Bush (1924-)*

From now on in America, any definition of a successful life must include serving others.
—*George Bush (1924-)*

Our deeds determine us, as much as we determine our deeds. —*George Eliot (1819–1880)*

Our deeds still travel with us from afar,
And what we have been makes us what we are.
—*George Eliot (1819–1880)*

What if my words were meant for deeds? —*George Eliot (1819–1880)*

It's not the cut of a man's coat, nor the manner of his dress. It's service that measures success.
—*George Washington Carver (1864–1943)*

A statesman is a politician who places himself at the service of the nation.
—*Georges Pompidou (1911–1974)*

I'm a determined person. And if I've got an objective, I'll make hours of sacrifice—whatever efforts are needed. —*Gerald Ford (1913-)*

I did not want simply to live or simply to live happily or well; I wanted to serve and do and make with some nobility. —*H. G. Wells (1866–1946)*

If you're not here to serve somebody, if there's going to be no integrity to your journey, no honor to it, then why are you here? —*Harry Belafonte (1927-)*

The really great men of earth are never known by their titled names, or seldom so, so significant has been their service, so distinguished their gifts, that their simple name is enough.
—*Harry Moyle Tippett (1891–1974)*

One of the difficulties with all our institutions is the fact that we've emphasized the reward instead of the service. —*Harry S Truman (1884–1972)*

Be not simply good; be good for something. —*Henry David Thoreau (1817–1862)*

One is not born into the world to do everything but to do something.
—*Henry David Thoreau* (1817–1862)

We judge ourselves by what we feel capable of doing, while others judge us by what we have already done.
—*Henry Wadsworth Longfellow (1807–1882)*

An idealist is a man who helps other men to be prosperous. . . . There is only one sure road to success—that is the road of service. Render a real service and fortune is sure to come to you.
—*Henry Ford (1863–1947)*

I have tried to live my life as my mother would have wished. She taught me as a boy that service is the highest duty in this world. I believed her then, and I believe her now. I have tried to follow her teaching. —*Henry Ford (1863–1947)*

There never was a person who did anything worth doing that did not receive more than he gave. —*Henry Ward Beecher (1813–1887)*

Help thy brother's boat across, and lo! thine own has reached the shore. —*Hindu Proverb*

The highest service we can perform for others is to help them help themselves. —*Horace Mann (1796–1859)*

Be ashamed to die until you have won some victory for humanity. —*Horace Mann (1796–1859)*

The world cannot always understand one's profession of faith, but it can understand service. —*Ian MacLaren (1850–1907)*

They helped every one his neighbor; and every one said to his brother, be of good courage. —*Isaiah 41:6*

We seldom stop to think how many peoples' lives are entwined with our own. It is a form of selfishness to imagine that every individual can operate on his own or can pull out of the general stream and not be missed. —*Ivy Baker Priest (1905–1975)*

You're born to serve the Lord and the brotherhood of man. It's everybody's obligation to help the least of our brethren. If that's right—and I think it is—then you have to work everyday to do that. —*J. Peter Grace (1913-)*

Service to youth is the rent we pay for the space we occupy on earth. —*Jane Deeter Rippin (1882–1953)*

As soon as public service ceases to be the chief business of the citizens, and they would rather serve with their money than with their persons, the State is not far from its fall. —*Jean Jacques Rousseau (1712–1778)*

It is in struggle and service with our brothers and sisters, individually and collectively, that we find the meaning of life. —*Jesse Jackson (1941-)*

The key to life is service to others. —*Jesse Jackson (1941-)*

We need a value system that will allow us to fulfill our essential human and humane tasks—to be producers, to be providers and to be protectors. —*Jesse Jackson (1941-)*

The only justification we have to look down on someone is because we are about to pick him up.
—*Jesse Jackson (1941-)*

Throughout my life, I've seen the difference that voluntary efforts can make in people's lives. I know the personal value of service as a local volunteer. —*Jimmy Carter (1924-)*

Act well at the moment, and you have performed a good action to all eternity.
—*Johann Kaspar Lavater (1741–1801)*

Individuals . . . make the decision to become involved . . . If they don't, they miss their most important chance to feel inner power and to become whole human beings. —*John D. Rockefeller, III (1906–1978)*

With a good conscience our only sure reward . . . let us go forth to lead the land we love . . . knowing that here on earth God's work must truly be our own. —*John F. Kennedy (1917–1963)*

You need a plan for everything, whether it's building a cathedral or a chicken coop. Without a plan, you'll postpone living until you're dead. —*John Goddard (1924-)*

When people are serving, life is no longer meaningless. —*John W. Gardner (1912-)*

Who soweth good seed shall surely reap. —*Julia C. Ripley Dorr (1825–1913)*

To survive, men and business and corporations must serve. —*John H. Patterson (1844–1922)*

I totally reject the view that the only business of business is business. The purpose of business is to serve society. —*Kenneth N. Dayton (1922-)*

The highest of distinctions is service to others. —*King George VI (1895–1952)*

The sole meaning of life is to serve humanity. —*Leo Tolstoy (1828–1910)*

The vocation of every man and woman is to serve other people. —*Leo Tolstoy (1828–1910)*

I prefer death to lassitude. I never tire of serving others. —*Leonardo da Vinci (1452–1519)*

You bring me the deepest joy that can be felt by a man whose invincible belief is that science and peace will triumph over ignorance and war, that nations will unite, not to destroy, but to build, and the future will belong to those who have done the most for suffering humanity. —*Louis Pasteur (1822–1895)*

That larger vision is certain to make clear the value in our own lives of service to others.
—*Lucy Larcom (1826–1893)*

Well-being is not found in isolation, possessions, or power itself; it usually appears while serving others. —*Manuel Arango (1936-)*

The role of a do-gooder is not what actors call a fat part. —*Margaret Halsey (1910-)*

Service is what life is all about; it never occurred to me not to be involved in the community. —*Marian Wright Edelman (1940-)*

To serve thy generation, this thy fate. . . .
But he who loves his kind does, first or late,
A work too great for fame.
—*Mary Clemmer Ames (1839–1884)*

The Son of Man came not to be served but to serve, and to give His life as a ransom for many. —*Matthew 20:28*

Put your hands to work, and your hearts to God. —*Mother Ann Lee (1736–1784)*

Duty is a very personal thing. It is what comes from knowing the need to take action and not just a need to urge others to do something. —*Mother Teresa (1910-)*

Man's greatest sin is not hatred, but indifference to one's brothers. —*Mother Teresa (1910-)*

All of us are but His instruments, who do our little bit and pass by. —*Mother Teresa (1910-)*

Wealth, position, fame, and even elusive happiness will be mine, eventually, if I determine to render more and better service, each day, than I am being paid to render. —*Og Mandino (1923-)*

Doing a 'good turn' may seem a trivial thing to us grown-ups, but a good turn done as a child will grow into service for the community when she grows up. —*Olave, Lady Baden-Powell (1889–1977)*

Every single one of us has the power for greatness, because greatness is determined by service—to yourself and to others. —*Oprah Winfrey (1954-)*

Fame has only the span of a day, they say. But to live in the hearts of the people—that is worth something. —*Ouida (1839–1908)*

Feed the flock of God; care for it willingly, not grudgingly; not for what you will get out of it, but because you are eager to serve the Lord. —*I Peter 5:2 (LB)*

One who lets slip by the opportunity to serve another, misses one of the richest experiences life has to offer. —*Pali Text*

The measure of a man is not in the number of his servants but in the number of people whom he serves.
—*Paul D. Moody (1779–1831)*

I have always recognized that the object of business is to make money in an honorable manner. I have endeavored to remember that the object of life is to do good. —*Peter Cooper (1791–1883)*

Each citizen should play his part in the community according to his individual gifts.
—*Plato (427–347 B.C.)*

I slept and dreamed that life was happiness. I awoke and saw that life was service. I served and found that in service happiness is found. —*Rabindranath Tagore (1861–1941)*

Almost anything can be bought for money—except the warm impulses of the human heart.
—*Ralph Waldo Emerson (1803–1882)*

Make yourself necessary to somebody. —*Ralph Waldo Emerson (1803–1882)*

When we try to serve or understand the world we touch what is divine. We get our dignity, our courage, our joy in work because of the greatness of the far-off and always in sight, always attainable, never at any moment attained. Service is one of the ways by which a tiny insect like one of us can get a purchase on the whole universe. If we find the job where we can be of use, we are hitched to the star of the world and move with it. —*Richard Clarke Cabot (1869–1939)*

Together, we can be twice as effective, twice as efficient, and twice as persuasive in helping solve this nation's serious social problems through community service. —*Richard F. Schubert (1936-)*

I am not called upon or expected to change any world except the one at the end of my fingertips.
—*Richard F. Schubert (1936-)*

I believe that serving and being served are reciprocal and that one cannot really be had without the other.
—*Robert K. Greenleaf (1904-1990)*

The ultimate test of servanthood is that those being served, by the way they are served, ultimately become disposed themselves to be servants. —*Robert K. Greenleaf (1904–1990)*

The most effective servants are those who can persuade others to go with them and who have learned to work in teams. —*Robert K. Greenleaf (1904-1990)*

Do your duty in all things. You could not do more; you should not wish to do less.
—*Robert E. Lee (1807–1870)*

If things are not going well with you, begin your effort at correcting the situation by carefully examining the service you are rendering, and especially the spirit in which you are rendering it.
—*Roger Babson (1875–1967)*

Present your bodies a living sacrifice, holy, acceptable unto God, which is your reasonable service. And be not conformed to this world: but be ye transformed by the renewing of your mind. —*Romans 12:1-2*

In this world everything changes except good deeds and bad deeds; these follow you as the shadow follows the body. —*Ruth Benedict (1887–1948)*

It is our first duty to serve society. —*Samuel Johnson (1709–1784)*

Find out where you can render a service, and then render it. The rest is up to the Lord.
—*Sebastian S. Kresge (1867–1966)*

The service we render to others is really the rent we pay for our room on this earth.
—*Sir Wilfred Grenfell (1865–1940)*

No man has a right to lead such a life of contemplation as to forget in his own ease the service due to his neighbor . . . —*St. Augustine (354–430)*

Grant us brotherhood, not only for this day but for all our years—a brotherhood not of words but of acts and deeds. —*Stephen Vincent Benet (1898–1943)*

In my career, I have learned that giving of your services for free gives you a good return on your investment, not just financially but morally. It supplements my personal integrity.
—*Stevie Wonder (1950-)*

To talk about doing good all day is not equal to doing one act of charity. If you do good and want people to know about it, then the good done becomes the root of evil. —*T. C. Lai (1921-)*

Men do less than they ought, unless they do all they can. —*Thomas Carlyle (1795–1881)*

The mystic bond of brotherhood makes all men one. —*Thomas Carlyle (1795–1881)*

I prefer to be remembered for what I have done for others, not what others have done for me.
—*Thomas Jefferson (1743–1826)*

Much has been given us, and much will rightfully be expected from us. We have duties to others and duties to ourselves; and we can shirk neither. —*Theodore Roosevelt (1858–1919)*

Our duty is to be useful—not according to our desires but according to our powers. —*Unknown*

The reward, the real grace of service is the opportunity not only to relieve suffering but to grow in wisdom, experience greater unity, and have a good time while doing it. —*Unknown*

Ten rules for getting rid of the blues: Go out and do something nice for someone else, then repeat it nine times. —*Unknown*

People will be happy in about the same degree that they are helpful. —*Unknown*

The world stands on three foundations—on study, on service and on benevolence. —*Unknown*

The greatest monument of a man is not a pyramid, but a record of service built upon a foundation of solid virtues: honesty, purpose, application, study, work, and kindliness. —*Unknown*

Service always is more eloquent than silence. —*Unknown*

Service is nothing but love in work clothes. —*Unknown*

Service isn't a big thing. It's a million little things. —*Unknown*

There is no success or happiness without service. —*Unknown*

There's no traffic jam on the extra mile. —*Unknown*

Life is like a game of tennis; the player who serves well seldom loses. —*Unknown*

In serving his vision of truth, the artist best serves his nation. —*Unknown*

It is through self-forgetting service to others that the highest self-fulfillment is realized.
—*V. Norskov Olsen (1916-)*

Give direction to my loving and my working so that my serving will make sense.
—*Virginia Talmadge (1914-)*

And now, humanity, I turn to you; I consecrate my service to the world!
—*Voltairine de Cleyre (1866–1912)*

Take a look at those two open hands of yours. They are tools with which to serve, make friends, and reach out for the best in life. Open hands open the way to achievement. Put them to work today.
—*Wilfred Peterson (1900-)*

Each of us will one day be judged by our standard of life—not by our standard of living; by our measure of giving—not by our measure of wealth, by our simple goodness—not by our seeming greatness.
—*William Arthur Ward (1921-)*

Blessed is the person who sees the need, recognizes the responsibility, and actively becomes the answer.
—*William Arthur Ward (1921-)*

Greatness is not found in possessions, power, position, or prestige. It is discovered in goodness, humility, service and character. —*William Arthur Ward (1921-)*

The great use of life is to spend it for something that outlasts it . —*William James (1842–1910)*

My heart is ever at your service. —*William Shakespeare (1564–1616)*

Let every man of whatsoever craft or occupation he be of . . . serve his brethren.
—*William Tyndale (1484–1536)*

Unless we take an active role in the lives of our communities, our communities will fail.
—*William Aramony (1927-)*

No man has ever risen to the real stature of spiritual manhood until he has found it is finer to serve somebody else than it is to serve himself. —*Woodrow Wilson (1856–1924)*

SOLICITING SUPPORT

Asking • Fund Raising • Philanthropy
Personal Contact • Friend Raising

We should never forget that no fund raising effort ever succeeds unless one person asks another person for money. *—Andrew D. Parker, Jr. (1943-)*

If you as askers do not give generously, could it be that that fact transmits itself unknowingly when you ask others to share? *—Arthur C. Frantzreb (1920-)*

People are generally better persuaded by the reasons which they have themselves discovered than by those which have come into the minds of others. *—Blaise Pascal (1623–1662)*

It's amazing what you don't get when you don't ask. *—Berney Neufeld (1941-)*

Raising money takes dogged persistence, bullheadedness, salesmanship, year-round cultivation, board support and encouragement, a plan, an attainable goal, and lots of excitement.
—Brian O'Connell (1930-)

A good fund raiser has the appetite of an IBM machine, the energy of a chimpanzee, the lungs of an umpire, the enthusiasm of a kid in an ice cream plant, and the shyness and timidity of a bull elephant.
—Charles H. Branch (1908-)

Fund raising is not an event; it is a process. *—Edgar D. Powell (1922–1984)*

Fund raising opportunities will continue to exist throughout the next century. Those opportunities will equal or exceed all current experience or presently held future expectations.
—Edgar D. Powell (1922–1984)

In fund raising, 95 percent is psychological or spiritual. Only 5 percent of it is financial. Actually, I don't ask for money. It's the other way around. People come to me and ask what they can do to help.
—*G. T. Smith (1935-)*

Always remember there is no "ceiling" on philanthropy . . . . In short: keep asking, keep raising sights, keep the "heat" on—because the money's there. —*George A. Brakeley, Jr. (1916-)*

People give to worthwhile programs rather than to needy institutions. The case must catch the eye, warm the heart and stir the mind. —*Harold J. Seymour (1894–1968)*

Remember that the best prospects are those who have already given and that the more a person gives, the more likely he is to give more. —*Harold J. Seymour (1894–1968)*

Fund raising is not a right — it is a privilege and we must always honor it as such.
—*Henry A. Rosso (1917-)*

The truly generous is the truly wise, and he who loves not others, lives unblest.
—*Henry Home (1696–1782)*

Fund raising requires both optimism and realism. Without the first, few if any gift solicitation efforts would be made. Without the second, few if any would succeed. —*Howard L. Jones (1917-)*

People support institutions which they perceive as reinforcing their own values.
—*James W. Frick (1924-)*

Large gifts, they are there for your organization. Men and women, waiting to be asked. Men and women, waiting for the right program, the proper motivation, the excitement and exhilaration of sharing in a great adventure. —*Jerold Panas (1928-)*

Blessed are the money raisers . . . for in heaven, they shall stand on the right hand of the martyrs.
—*John R. Mott (1865–1955)*

If you don't get the funding sources out to where the action is, funds will soon dry up because the sources' interest had never been whetted. —*John W. Hechinger (1920-)*

Personal contact will accomplish ten times what a cold letter will. Use that personal touch!
—*John J. Wilson (1917-)*

If you will please people, you must please them in their own way. —*Lord Chesterfield (1694–1773)*

And all things, whatsoever ye shall ask in prayer, believing, ye shall receive. —*Matthew 21:22*

Ask, and it shall be given you; seek, and ye shall find. —*Matthew 7:7*

If you want money, ask for advice. If you want advice, ask for money. —*Modern Fund Raising Maxim*

Money-getters are the benefactors of our race. To them . . . are we indebted for our institutions of learning, and of art, our academies, colleges and churches. —*P. T. Barnum (1810–1891)*

Make no mistake, asking is the heart of the matter. . . . Many people actually look forward to it. Being asked helps to satisfy the human need to be wanted, to be courted. —*Paul H. Schneiter (1935-)*

Philanthropic dollars are not free. They have to be earned—with excellence and performance, with patience and long suffering. —*Paul H. Schneiter (1935-)*

Philanthropy is the one institution in America, even beyond education, that has a sixth sense of how to recognize and exploit human creativity. —*Paul N. Ylvisaker (1921-)*

When asked by a prospective donor how much he should give, the best reply is, "Give until you are proud." —*Paul Ireland (1914–1987)*

Be generous, and you will be prosperous. Help others, and you will be helped. —*Proverbs 11:25 (GNB)*

Be generous and share your food with the poor. You will be blessed for it. —*Proverbs 22:9 (LB)*

There are no bad fund raisers and there are no bad fund raising campaigns. There are only bad visions and dreams. —*Robert H. Schuller (1926-)*

When someone gives the hospital a gift of $5 and you know he can afford less than that, thank him profusely. When someone gives the hospital a gift of $5,000 and you know he could afford five times that, say "that will help." —*Robert H. Thorson (1916-)*

The record of a generous life runs like a vine around the memory of our dead, and every sweet unselfish act is now a perfumed flower. —*Robert G. Ingersoll (1833–1899)*

Fund raising is a matter of presence and timing, and if you've got the presence you can guess the timing. —*Sheree Parris Nudd (1954-)*

When we recognize that a better word for fund raising is "friend raising," we open limitless doors to creativity in support of our causes. —*Sue Vineyard (1938-)*

Let him who wants to move and convince others, be first moved and convinced himself. —*Thomas Carlyle (1795–1881)*

Money is not given, it has to be raised. Money is not offered, it has to be asked for. Money does not come in, It must be "gone after." —*Unknown*

People support what they help create. —*Unknown*

We don't always get what we deserve, but we often get what we ask for. —*Victor G. Dymowski (1944-)*

Generous deeds would be repeated oftener if more gratitude had been shown for the first ones. —*William Feather (1870–1944)*

SUCCESS
Work • Enthusiasm • Service
Excellence • Vision

If we could sell our experiences for what they cost us, we'd all be millionaires.
—*Abigail Van Buren (1918-)*

If you want a place in the sun, you've got to put up with a few blisters. —*Abigail Van Buren (1918-)*

Let no feeling of discouragement prey upon you, and in the end you are sure to succeed.
—*Abraham Lincoln (1809–1865)*

The probability that we may fail in the struggle ought not to deter us from the support of a cause we believe to be just. —*Abraham Lincoln (1809–1865)*

There is dignity in work only when it is work freely accepted. —*Albert Camus (1913–1960)*

Only those who attempt the absurd will achieve the impossible. —*Albert Einstein (1879–1955)*

It is high time the ideal of success should be replaced with the ideal of service.
—*Albert Einstein (1879–1955)*

One hundred times a day I remind myself that my personal and professional . . . life depends on the fruit of the work of other men, living and dead, . . . and that I should make every effort to give in the same measure in which I have received and am receiving. —*Albert Einstein (1879–1955)*

No ray of sunlight is ever lost, but the green that it wakes needs time to sprout, and it is not always granted to the sower to see the harvest. All work that is worth anything is done in faith.
—*Albert Schweitzer (1875–1965)*

Experience is not what happens to a man, it is what a man does with what happens to him. It is a gift for dealing with the accidents of existence, not the accidents themselves. —*Aldous Huxley (1894–1963)*

Nothing succeeds like success. —*Alexandre Dumas (1802–1870)*

The wealth of a democratic society may be measured by the quality of functions performed by private citizens. —*Alexis de Tocqueville (1805–1859)*

Ideas won't keep. Something has to be done about them. —*Alfred North Whitehead (1861–1947)*

A man cannot live off his community; he must live in it. —*Amon G. Carter, Sr. (1879–1955)*

To accomplish great things, we must not only act but also dream, not only plan but also believe. —*Anatole France (1844–1924)*

Work! Thank God for the might of it,
The ardor, the urge, the delight of it.
—*Angela Morgan (1873–1957)*

Opportunities are usually disguised as hard work, so most people don't recognize them. —*Ann Landers (1918-)*

If we do not do the work we were meant to do, it will forever remain undone. —*Anna Lindsay (1864–1948)*

Laziness may appear attractive, but work gives satisfaction. —*Anne Frank (1929–1945)*

The only way to achieve true success is to express yourself completely in service to society. —*Aristotle (384-322 B.C.)*

There have been men and women in every generation who have longed for a better day and who have been willing to aid the forces which they believed would hasten that day. —*Arnaud C. Marts (1888–1970)*

I believe in the "No Deposit, No Return" statement: unless we put into the American privilege of freedom of choice, we can expect no return; indeed, we have no right of return. —*Arthur C. Frantzreb (1920-)*

The roots of excellence are the freedom to dream the unthinkable and to finance the impossible. —*Arthur C. Frantzreb (1920-)*

You've got to know where it is and go after it. You won't get it every time, but it's worth trying. —*Arthur C. Frantzreb (1920-)*

Success in life should be determined by contributions, not accumulations. —*Arthur F. Lenehan (1921-)*

The ladder of success is best climbed by stepping on the rungs of opportunity. —*Ayn Rand (1905–1982)*

It's no use waiting for your ship to come in, unless you've sent one out. —*Belgian Proverb*

I think of success as reaching beyond ourselves and helping other people in specific ways.
—*Ben Carson (1951-)*

What is important—what I consider success—is that we make a contribution to our world.
—*Ben Carson (1951-)*

The secret of success in life is for a man to be ready for his opportunity when it comes.
—*Benjamin Disraeli (1804–1881)*

The secret of success is constancy to purpose. —*Benjamin Disraeli (1804–1881)*

Never explain, never retract, never apologize—get the thing done and let them howl!
—*Benjamin Jowett (1817–1893)*

This became a credo of mine . . . attempt the impossible in order to improve your work.
—*Bette Davis (1908–1989)*

You may be disappointed if you fail, but you are doomed if you don't try. —*Beverly Sills (1929-)*

There's no labor a man can do that's undignified—if he does it right. —*Bill Cosby (1937-)*

I believe that any man's life will be filled with constant and unexpected encouragement, if he makes up his mind to do his level best each day, and as nearly as possible reach the high-water mark of pure and useful living. —*Booker T. Washington (1856–1915)*

Success is not measured by the heights one attains, but by the obstacles one overcomes in its attainment.
—*Booker T. Washington (1856–1915)*

No man can persuade people to do what he wants them to do unless he genuinely likes people, and believes that what he wants them to do is to their own advantage. —*Bruce Barton (1886–1967)*

Every man's work shall be made manifest. —*I Corinthians 3:13*

Nothing in the world can take the place of persistence. Talent will not; nothing is more common than unsuccessful men with talent. Genius will not; unrewarded genius is almost a proverb. Education will not; the world is full of educated derelicts. Persistence and determination alone are omnipotent.
—*Calvin Coolidge (1872–1933)*

Never be afraid to take on a really tough problem. When you solve it, the benefits will be that much greater.
—*Carl A. Gerstacker (1916-)*

It all depends on how we look at things, and not on how they are. —*Carl Gustav Jung (1875–1964)*

Experience shows that success is due less to ability than to zeal. The winner is he who gives himself to his work, body, and soul. —*Charles Buxton (1823–1871)*

Nothing great will ever be achieved without great men, and men are great only if they are determined to be so. —*Charles de Gaulle (1890–1970)*

Every failure teaches a man something if he will learn. —*Charles Dickens (1812–1870)*

A good boss is one who makes his men think they have more ability than they have, so they consistently do better work than they thought they could. —*Charles E. Wilson (1890–1961)*

Keep on going and the chances are you will stumble on something, perhaps when you are least expecting it. I have never heard of anyone stumbling on something sitting down.
—*Charles F. Kettering (1876–1958)*

The greatest thing this generation can do is to lay a few stepping stones for the next generation.
—*Charles F. Kettering (1876–1958)*

If I have had any success, it's due to luck, but I notice the harder I work, the luckier I get.
—*Charles F. Kettering (1876–1958)*

Nothing ever built arose to touch the skies unless some man dreamed that it should, some man believed that it could, and some man willed that it must. —*Charles F. Kettering (1876–1958)*

Failures, repeated failures, are finger posts on the road to achievement. One fails forward toward success.
—*Charles F. Kettering (1876–1958)*

The person who doesn't know something can't be done will often find a way to go ahead and do it.
—*Charles F. Kettering (1876–1958)*

What I believe is that, by proper effort, we make the future almost anything we want to make it.
—*Charles F. Kettering (1876–1958)*

Take good care of your future because that's where you're going to spend the rest of your life. —*Charles F. Kettering (1876–1958)*

When a man has put a limit on what he will do, he has put a limit on what he can do. —*Charles M. Schwab (1862–1939)*

Work hard. Hard work is the best investment a man can make. —*Charles M. Schwab (1862–1939)*

We are all salesmen every day of our lives. We are selling our ideas, our plans, our enthusiasms to those with whom we come in contact. —*Charles M. Schwab (1862–1939)*

Help and share with others. The real test of business greatness lies in giving opportunities to others. —*Charles M. Schwab (1862–1939)*

In all things do your best. The man who has done his best has done everything. The man who has done less than his best has done nothing. —*Charles M. Schwab (1862–1939)*

Learning is like rowing upstream: not to advance is to drop back. —*Chinese Proverb*

If you are planning for a year, plant grain. If you are planning for a decade, plant trees. If you are planning for a century, plant men. — *Chinese Proverb*

Be not disturbed at being misunderstood; be disturbed rather at not being understanding. —*Chinese Proverb*

He who sacrifices his conscience to ambition burns a picture to obtain ashes. —*Chinese Proverb*

Self-image determines self-esteem, self-esteem determines priorities, and priorities determine success. Improve the world by doing those things which legitimately boost your self-image and that of others. —*Clarence E. Hodges (1939-)*

Your best appearance may be what is most remembered about you; don't leave home without it. —*Clarence E. Hodges (1939-)*

Your integrity will affect your destiny; don't leave home without it. —*Clarence E. Hodges (1939-)*

It doesn't make sense to talk about successful corporations in a society whose schools, hospitals, churches, symphonies, or libraries are deteriorating or closing. —*Clifton C. Garvin, Jr. (1921-)*

How many cares one loses when one decides not to be something, but to be someone. —*Coco Chanel (1883–1971)*

There are no secrets to success. It is the result of preparation, hard work, and learning from failure. —*Colin L. Powell (1937-)*

Hard work beats all the tonics and vitamins in the world. —*Colonel Sanders (1890–1980)*

Whatsoever you do, do it heartily, as to the Lord and not unto men. —*Colossians 3:23 (NKJV)*

Success can make you go one of two ways. It can make you a prima donna, or it can smooth the edges, take away the insecurities, let the nice things come out. —*Cynthia Ozick (1928-)*

If only I may grow: firmer, simpler—quieter, warmer. —*Dag Hammarskjold (1905–1961)*

You can make more friends in two months by becoming really interested in other people, than you can in two years by trying to get other people interested in you. —*Dale Carnegie (1888–1955)*

If you must make a mistake, make a new one each time. —*Dale Carnegie (1888–1955)*

Take a chance! All life is a chance. The man who goes furthest is generally the one who is willing to do and dare. —*Dale Carnegie (1888–1955)*

Make no little plans, they have no magic to stir men's blood. . . . Make big plans, aim high in hope and work, remembering that noble, logical diagram. . . will be a living thing, asserting itself with ever growing insistence. —*Daniel H. Burnham*

All of us are born for a reason, but all of us don't discover why. Success in life has nothing to do with what you gain in life or accomplish for yourself. It's what you do for others. —*Danny Thomas (1914–1991)*

I am willing to go anywhere, anywhere, anywhere—so long as it's forward. —*David Livingston (1813–1873)*

Don't be afraid to take a big step. You can't cross a chasm in two small jumps. —*David Lloyd George (1863–1945)*

Let us realize that the privilege to work is a gift, that power to work is a blessing, that love of work is success. —*David O. McKay (1873–1970)*

Goals are as essential to success as air is to life. —*David Schwartz (1916-)*

Determine your future now by taking hold of every opportunity. —*Debbye Turner (1965-)*

The winners in life think constantly in terms of I can, I will and I am. Losers, on the other hand, concentrate their waking thoughts on what they should have or would have done, or what they don't do. —*Denis Waitley (1933-)*

The dream is not the destination but the journey. —*Diane Sawyer (1945-)*

Time is the most precious gift in our possession, for it is the most irrevocable. —*Dietrich Bonhoeffer (1906–1945)*

One cannot make oneself, but one can sometimes help a little in the making of somebody else. —*Dinah Mulock Craik (1826–1887)*

The way I see it, if you want the rainbow, you gotta put up with the rain. —*Dolly Parton (1946-)*

You set a goal to be the best and then you work hard every hour of every day, striving to reach that goal. If you allow yourself to settle for anything less than number one, you are cheating yourself. —*Don Shula (1930-)*

Any human anywhere will blossom in a hundred unexpected talents and capacities simply by being given the opportunity to do so. — *Doris Lessing (1919-)*

There is no security on this earth. There is only opportunity. —*Douglas MacArthur (1880–1964)*

A people that values its privileges above its principles soon loses both. —*Dwight D. Eisenhower (1890–1969)*

It is ability, not disability that counts. —*Edgar J. Helmes (1863–1942)*

Every man should make up his mind that if he expects to succeed, he must give an honest return for the other man's dollar. —*Edward H. Harriman (1848–1909)*

Your dream might change our planet. —*Edward Lindaman (1920–1982)*

Too low they build who build beneath the stars. —*Edward Young (1681–1765)*

Do your work with your whole heart and you will succeed—there is so little competition! —*Elbert Hubbard (1856–1915)*

There are two kinds of people in the world—those who are always getting ready to do something, and those who go ahead and do it. —*Elbert Hubbard (1856–1915)*

There is a wild, splendid, intoxicating joy that follows work well done. —*Elbert Hubbard (1856–1915)*

We work to become, not to acquire. —*Elbert Hubbard (1856–1915)*

The pathway to success is in serving humanity. By no other means is it possible, and this truth is so plain and patent that even very simple folk recognize it. —*Elbert Hubbard (1856–1915)*

As individuals we live cooperatively, and, to the best of our ability, serve the community in which we live. Our own success, to be real, must contribute to the success of others.
—*Eleanor Roosevelt (1884–1962)*

The thing which counts is the striving of the human soul to achieve spiritually the best that it is capable of and to care unselfishly not only for personal good, but for the good of all those who toil with them upon the earth. —*Eleanor Roosevelt (1884–1962)*

The future belongs to those who believe in the beauty of their dreams.
—*Eleanor Roosevelt (1884–1962)*

You have to accept whatever comes and the only important thing is that you meet it with courage and with the best you have to give. —*Eleanor Roosevelt (1884–1962)*

You must do the thing you think you cannot do. —*Eleanor Roosevelt (1884–1962)*

Just as there are no little people or unimportant lives, there is no insignificant work.
—*Elena Bonner (1923-)*

Let us be content to work, to do the thing we can, and not presume to fret because it is little.
—*Elizabeth Barrett Browning (1806–1861)*

Let us not wait a moment. Let each of us work to build organizations where everyone can make a contribution . . . where everybody counts . . . organizations which will continue to change the world.
—*Elizabeth Dole (1936-)*

Material possessions will rust away, wear away, or depreciate—but your inner resources—character— must never depreciate. In seeking success you must also seek fulfillment. Ask yourself not only what you want to be, but who you want to be. —*Elizabeth Dole (1936-)*

There is no chance, no destiny, no fate, can circumvent or hinder, or control, the firm resolve of a determined soul. —*Ella Wheeler Wilcox (1855–1919)*

God gives opportunities; success depends upon the use made of them. —*Ellen G. White (1827–1915)*

Success is counted sweetest by those who ne'er succeed. —*Emily Dickinson (1830–1886)*

Where there's a will, there's a way. —*English Proverb*

And the trouble is if you don't risk anything, you risk even more. —*Erica Jong (1942-)*

All serious daring starts from within. —*Eudora Welty (1909-)*

To convert ideas and good intentions into something real and positive requires time and perseverance.
—*Eugenio Mendoza (1906–1979)*

The most powerful weapon on earth is the human soul on fire. —*Ferdinand Foch (1859–1929)*

Labor is the source of all wealth and all culture. —*Ferdinand Lassalle (1825–1864)*

The failure to be perfect does not mean you are not a success; it is giving your best that helps you to understand the joy of receiving. —*Fran Tarkenton (1940-)*

Before strongly desiring anything, we should look carefully into the happiness of its present owner.
—*Francois de la Rochefoucauld (1613–1680)*

When you get to the end of your rope, tie a knot and hang on. —*Franklin D. Roosevelt (1882–1945)*

Progress always involves risk. You can't steal second base and keep your foot on first.
—*Frederick B. Wilcox (1879–1965)*

Greatness is not standing above our fellows and ordering them around—it is standing with them and helping them to be all they can be. —*G. Arthur Keough (1909–1989)*

I learned that if you want to make it bad enough, no matter how bad it is, you can make it.
—*Gale Sayers (1943-)*

To succeed in life one must have determination and must be prepared to suffer during the process. If one isn't prepared to suffer during adversities, I don't really see how he can be successful.
—*Gary Player (1935-)*

Life is a sort of splendid torch which I've got hold of for the moment and I want to make it burn as brightly as possible before handing it on to future generations. —*George Bernard Shaw (1856–1950)*

Life is no 'brief candle' to me. I want to be thoroughly used up when I die, for the harder I work the more I live. —*George Bernard Shaw (1856–1950)*

The strongest principle of growth is human choice. —*George Eliot (1819–1880)*

It is never too late to be what you might have been. —*George Eliot (1819–1880)*

Accept the challenges, so that you may feel the exhilaration of victory. —*George Patton (1885–1945)*

Work is not man's punishment. It is his reward and strength, his glory and his pleasure.
—*George Sand (1804–1876)*

We must never despair; our situation has been compromising before. . . If new difficulties arise, we must put forth new exertion and proportion our efforts to the exigencies of the times.
—*George Washington (1732–1799)*

Ninety-nine percent of the failures come from people who have the habit of making excuses.
—*George Washington Carver (1864–1943)*

How far you go in life depends on your being tender with the young, compassionate with the aged, sympathetic with the striving and tolerant of the weak and the strong.
—*George Washington Carver (1864–1943)*

To me, success is not something to be measured in power or fortune or fame. I believe a life of service to others is a successful life. —*Gerald R. Ford (1913-)*

Always demanding the best of oneself, living with honor, devoting one's talents and gifts to the benefit of others—these are the measures of success that endure when material things have passed away.
—*Gerald R. Ford (1913-)*

A difference, to be a difference, must make a difference. —*Gertrude Stein (1874–1946)*

I can honestly say that I was never affected by the questions of the success of an undertaking. If I felt it was the right thing to do, I was for it regardless of the possible outcome. —*Golda Meir (1898–1979)*

The common tasks are beautiful if we have eyes to see their shining ministry.
—*Grace Noll Crowell (1877–1969)*

Before you can score, you must first have a goal. —*Greek Proverb*

You can work at something for twenty years and come away with twenty years' worth of valuable experience, or you can come away with one year's experience twenty times. —*Gwen Jackson (1928-)*

Success is to be measured not by wealth, power, or fame, but by the ratio between what a man is and what he might be. —*H. G. Wells (1866–1946)*

It is by surmounting difficulties, not by sinking under them that we discover our fortitude.
—*Hannah Webster Foster (1758–1840)*

We will either find a way, or make one. —*Hannibal (247–182 B.C.)*

It approaches neglect if an organization could make an intensive and successful effort to secure major gifts and fails to do so. —*Harold D. Wilkins (1929-)*

When you get into a tight place and everything goes against you until it seems as though you cannot hold on for a minute longer, never give up then, for that is just the place and time that the tide will turn.
—*Harriet Beecher Stowe (1811–1896)*

A man cannot leave a better legacy to the world than a well-educated family.
—*Harry S Truman (1884–1972)*

Since many of you work in this arena where return on investment is the prime criteria for success, I want to give you a tip. Start immediately giving away at least 10 percent of your income, no matter what your income is, because this will ensure that your family will never want. . . . And then if you learn to give away 15 to 20 percent and more, you'll really start to get rich. —*Harvey Enchin (1937-)*

It is only as we develop others that we permanently succeed. —*Harvey S. Firestone (1868–1938)*

I am only one; but still I am one. I cannot do everything, but still I can do something; I will not refuse to do the something I can do. —*Helen Keller (1880–1968)*

The world is moved not only by the mighty shoves of the heroes, but also by the aggregate of the tiny pushes of each honest worker. —*Helen Keller (1880–1968)*

Keep your face to the sunshine and you cannot see the shadow. —*Helen Keller (1880–1968)*

Worse than being blind would be to be able to see but not have any vision. —*Helen Keller (1880–1968)*

If one advances confidently in the direction of his dreams, and endeavors to live the life which he has imagined, he will meet with a success unexpected in common hours.
—*Henry David Thoreau (1817–1862)*

When everything seems to be going against you, remember that the airplane takes off against the wind, not with it. —*Henry Ford (1863–1947)*

You can do anything if you have enthusiasm. . . . Enthusiasm is at the bottom of all progress. With it, there is accomplishment. Without it, there are only alibis. —*Henry Ford (1863–1947)*

Failure is only the opportunity to begin again, more intelligently. —*Henry Ford (1863–1947)*

Before everything else, getting ready is the secret of success. —*Henry Ford (1863–1947)*

Success is . . . a matter of adjusting one's efforts to obstacles and one's abilities to a service needed by others. . . . Most people think of it in terms of getting; success, however, begins in terms of giving. —*Henry Ford (1863–1947)*

Let no man imagine that he has no influence. Whoever he may be, and wherever he may be placed, the man who thinks becomes a light and a power. —*Henry George (1862–1916)*

Remember that what you possess in the world will be found at the day of your death to belong to another, but what you are will be yours forever. —*Henry Van Dyke (1852–1933)*

The talent of success is nothing more than doing what you can do well, and doing well whatever you do, without a thought of fame. —*Henry Wadsworth Longfellow (1807–1882)*

Lives of great men all remind us that we can make our lives sublime, and departing, leave behind us footprints on the sands of time. —*Henry Wadsworth Longfellow (1807–1882)*

I cannot give you the formula for success, but I can give you the formula for failure, which is—try to please everybody. —*Herbert Bayard Swope (1882–1958)*

The structure of human betterment cannot be built upon foundations of materialism or business, but upon the bedrock of individual character in free men and women. —*Herbert C. Hoover (1874–1964)*

Failure is only postponed success as long as courage 'coaches' ambition. The habit of persistence is the habit of victory. —*Herbert Kaufman (1922-)*

Men are often capable of greater things than they perform. They are sent into the world with bills of credit, and seldom draw to their full extent. —*Horace Walpole (1717–1797)*

The work of the individual still remains the spark that moves mankind ahead. —*Igor Sikorsky (1889–1972)*

The only people who fail are those who never try. —*Ilka Chase (1905–1978)*

My grandfather once told me that there are two kinds of people; those who do the work and those who take the credit. He told me to try to be in the first group; there was less competition there. —*Indira Gandhi (1917–1984)*

We must learn to be still in the midst of activity and to be vibrantly alive in repose.
—*Indira Gandhi (1917–1984)*

If God shuts one door, He opens another. —*Irish Proverb*

You've got to do your own growing, no matter how tall your grandfather was. —*Irish Proverb*

The toughest thing about success is that you've got to keep on being a success.
—*Irving Berlin (1888–1989)*

Life is 10 percent what you make it and 90 percent how you take it. —*Irving Berlin (1888–1989)*

The optimist thinks this is the best of all possible worlds, and the pessimist knows it.
—*J. Robert Oppenheimer (1904–1967)*

The world is before you, and you need not take it or leave it as it was when you came in.
—*James Baldwin (1924–1987)*

When a man forgets himself, he usually does something everybody else remembers.
—*James Coco (1929–1987)*

It is right to be contented with what we have, never with what we are. —*James Mackintosh (1765–1832)*

Don't compromise yourself. You're all you've got. —*Janis Joplin (1943–1970)*

A journey of a thousand miles begins with one step. —*Japanese Proverb*

Our chief defect is that we are more given to talking about things than to doing them.
—*Jawaharlal Nehru (1889–1964)*

Loyal and efficient work in a great cause, even though it may not be immediately recognized, ultimately bears fruit. —*Jawaharlal Nehru (1889–1964)*

If you want to innovate, to change an enterprise or a society, it takes people willing to do what's not expected. —*Jean Riboud (1919-)*

We cannot work for others without working for ourselves. —*Jean-Jacques Rousseau (1712–1778)*

I don't think success is harmful, as so many people say. Rather, I believe it indispensable to talent, if for nothing else than to increase the talent. —*Jeanne Moreau (1929-)*

Excellence is never an accident. —*Jerold Panas (1928-)*

If we are to lift ourselves out of this morass, we must shift our sights from the superficial to the sacrificial.
—*Jesse Jackson (1941-)*

A slave is a free man if he is content with his lot; a free man is a slave if he seeks more than that.
—*Jewish Proverb*

To be successful, you don't have to do extraordinary things. Just do ordinary things extraordinarily well.
—*Jim Rohn (1930-)*

Success without honor is an unseasoned dish; it will satisfy your hunger, but it won't taste good.
—*Joe Paterno (1926-)*

What you have inherited from your fathers, earn over again for yourselves, or it will not be yours.
—*Johann Wolfgang von Goethe (1749–1832)*

I wish above all things that thou mayest prosper and be in health, even as thy soul prospereth.
—*III John 2*

You don't ask a juggler which ball is highest in priority. Success is to do it all.
—*John Armstrong (1934-)*

If you want to succeed you should strike out on new paths rather than travel the worn paths of accepted success. —*John D. Rockefeller (1839–1937)*

Who hath not served cannot command. —*John Florio (1553–1625)*

Success lies in doing not what others consider to be great but what you consider to be right.
—*John Gray (1839–1915)*

The tissue of the life to be
We weave with colors all our own,
And in the field of destiny
We reap as we have sown.
—*John Greenleaf Whittier (1807–1892)*

Quality is never an accident; it is always the result of intelligent effort. —*John Ruskin (1819–1900)*

The highest reward for man's toil is not what he gets for it, but what he becomes by it. —*John Ruskin (1819–1900)*

All excellence involves discipline and tenacity of purpose. —*John W. Gardner (1912-)*

The idea for which this nation stands will not survive if the highest goal that free men can set for themselves is an amiable mediocrity. —*John W. Gardner (1912-)*

The prospects never looked brighter and the problems never looked tougher. Anyone who isn't stirred by both of those statements is too tired to be of much use to us in the days ahead. —*John W. Gardner (1912-)*

Courage is being scared to death—and saddling up anyway. —*John Wayne (1907–1979)*

Success is a peace of mind which is a direct result of self-satisfaction in knowing that you did your best to become the best you are capable of becoming. —*John Wooden (1910-)*

I could not wait for success, so I went ahead without it. —*Jonathan Winters (1925-)*

Making anything a success rests with people and commitment, strong will to always do the best, confidence in one another . . . and absolute determination. —*Jorgen Roed (1935-)*

Don't let your life be sterile. Be useful. Blaze a trail. Shine forth with the light of your faith and of your love. —*Jose Maria Escriva (1902–1975)*

Imagination, not invention, is the supreme master of art as of life. —*Joseph Conrad (1857–1924)*

The future is not in the hands of fate, but in ours. —*Jules Jusserand (1855–1932)*

Perseverance is failing nineteen times and succeeding the twentieth. —*Julie Andrews (1935-)*

Work is love made visible. And if you cannot work with love but only with distaste, it is better that you should leave your work and sit at the gate of the temple and take alms of those who work with joy. —*Kahlil Gibran (1883–1931)*

To love what you do and feel that it matters—how could anything be more fun? —*Katherine Meyer Graham (1917-)*

I do not want to die . . . until I have faithfully made the most of my talent and cultivated the seed that was placed in me until the last small twig has grown. —*Kathe Kollwitz (1867–1945)*

There is no failure except in no longer trying. There is no defeat except from within; no really insurmountable barrier save our own inherent weakness of purpose. —*Ken Hubbard (1868–1930)*

There's a difference between interest and commitment. When you're interested in doing something, you do it only when it's convenient. When you're committed to something, you accept no excuses, only results. —*Kenneth Blanchard (1939-)*

Each one of us can work for a small change in the world around us. —*Lamar S. Smith (1947-)*

Management is nothing more than motivating other people. —*Lee Iacocca (1924-)*

Work is the inevitable condition of human life, the true source of human welfare. —*Leo Tolstoy (1828–1910)*

Time stays long enough for anyone who will use it. —*Leonardo da Vinci (1452–1519)*

A strong determination to get the best out of life, a keen desire to enjoy what one has, and no regrets if one fails: this is the secret of the Chinese genius for contentment. —*Lin Yutang (1895–1976)*

Don't do nothing halfway, else you find yourself dropping more than can be picked up. —*Louis Armstrong (1900–1971)*

Victory is won not in miles but in inches. Win a little now, hold your ground, and later win a little more. —*Louis L'Amour (1908–1988)*

In human endeavor, chance favors the prepared mind. —*Louis Pasteur (1822–1895)*

Make each day useful and cheerful and prove that you know the worth of time by employing it well. Then youth will be happy, old age without regret and life a beautiful success. —*Louisa May Alcott (1832–1888)*

Far away there in the sunshine are my highest aspirations. I may not reach them, but I can look up and see their beauty, believe in them and try to follow where they lead. —*Louisa May Alcott (1832–1888)*

Luck? I don't know anything about luck. I've never banked on it, and I'm afraid of people who do. Luck to me is something else: hard work—and realizing what is opportunity and what isn't. —*Lucille Ball (1911–1989)*

One of the things I learned the hard way was that it doesn't pay to get discouraged. Keeping busy and making optimism a way of life can restore your faith in yourself. —*Lucille Ball (1911–1989)*

For is it not true that human progress is but a mighty growing pattern woven together by the tenuous single threads united in a common effort? —*Madame Chiang Kai-Shek (1898-)*

Monotony is the law of nature. Look at the monotonous manner in which the sun rises. The monotony of necessary occupations is exhilarating and life-giving. —*Mahatma Gandhi (1869–1948)*

Too many people overvalue what they're not and undervalue what they are.
—*Malcolm S. Forbes (1919–1990)*

It's always worthwhile to make others aware of their worth. —*Malcolm S. Forbes (1919–1990)*

At the heart of any good business is a chief executive officer with one.
—*Malcolm S. Forbes (1919–1990)*

Our business in life is not to get ahead of other people, but to get ahead of ourselves.
—*Maltbie D. Babcock (1858–1901)*

Work is the world's easiest escape from boredom and the only surefire road to success.
—*Marabel Morgan (1937-)*

I have lost when I have not the bright feeling of progression. —*Margaret Fuller (1810–1850)*

Success is having a flair for the thing you are doing while knowing that it is not enough. You have got to have hard work and a certain sense of purpose. —*Margaret Thatcher (1925-)*

As long as you keep putting a person down, you cannot soar as you otherwise might.
—*Marian Anderson (1902-)*

I was taught that the way of progress is neither swift nor easy. —*Marie Curie (1867–1934)*

Life is not easy for any of us. But what of that? We must have perseverance and above all confidence in ourselves. We must believe that we are gifted for something, and that this thing, at whatever cost, must be attained. —*Marie Curie (1867–1934)*

One never notices what has been done; one can only see what remains to be done.
—*Marie Curie (1867–1934)*

The distance is nothing; it is only the first step that is difficult.
—*Marie de Vichy-Chamrond (1697–1780)*

No one is so eager to gain new experience as he who doesn't know how to make use of the old ones.
—*Marie Ebner von Eschenbach (1830–1916)*

And whosoever of you will be the chiefest, shall be the servant of all. —*Mark 10:44*

The ladder of life is full of splinters, but they always prick the hardest when we're sliding down.
—*Mark Twain (1835–1910)*

Bring ideas in and entertain them royally, for one of them may be the king.
—*Mark Van Doren (1894–1972)*

Aerodynamically the bumble bee shouldn't be able to fly, but the bumble bee doesn't know it so it goes on flying anyway. —*Mary Kay Ash*

You can do anything in this world you want to do if you want to do it badly enough—and you are willing to pay the price! —*Mary Kay Ash*

If excellence is to prevail in our lives, mediocrity must be shunned at every cost.
—*Mary Louise Wiley (1958-)*

Seek ye first the kingdom of God, and his righteousness; and all these things shall be added unto you.
—*Matthew 6:33*

We, whoever we are, must have a daily goal in our lives, no matter how small or great, to make that day mean something. —*Maxwell Maltz (1899-)*

Excellence costs a great deal. —*May Sarton (1912-)*

Our greatest strength comes not from what we possess but from what we believe, not from what we have, but from who we are. —*Michael S. Dukakis (1933-)*

If people knew how hard I have to work to gain my mastery, it wouldn't seem wonderful at all.
—*Michelangelo (1475–1564)*

Lord, grant that I may always desire more than I can accomplish. —*Michelangelo (1475–1564)*

The objective is not to pass, but to surpass. —*Millie Thornton (1958-)*

Success is measured not by what you get but rather by what you give. —*Mitzi Perdue (1941-)*

Our work brings people face to face with love. —*Mother Teresa (1910-)*

It is an achievement for a man to do his duty on earth irrespective of the consequences.
—*Nelson Mandela (1918-)*

A prudent man should always follow in the path trodden by great men and imitate those who are most excellent. —*Niccolo Machiavelli (1469–1527)*

Progress begins with the belief that what is necessary is possible. —*Norman Cousins (1912-)*

The man who lives for himself is a failure. Even if he gains much wealth, position or fortune, he is still a failure. The man who lives for others has achieved true success. A rich man who consecrates his wealth and his position to the good of humanity is a success. —*Norman Vincent Peale (1898–1993)*

Think success, visualize success, and you will set in motion the power force of the realizable wish.
—*Norman Vincent Peale (1898–1993)*

One person can make a difference. . . . You don't have to be a big shot. You don't have to have a lot of influence. You just have to have faith in your power to change things.
—*Norman Vincent Peale (1898–1993)*

My days of whining and complaining about others have come to an end. Nothing is easier than fault-finding. All it will do is discolor my personality so that none will want to associate with me. That was my old life. No more. —*Og Mandino (1923-)*

Our greatest glory consists not in never failing, but in rising every time we fall.
—*Oliver Goldsmith (1728–1774)*

I attempt a difficult work; but there is no excellence without difficulty. —*Ovid (43 B.C.–17 A.D.)*

The secret of joy is contained in one word—excellence. To know how to do something well is to enjoy it.
—*Pearl S. Buck (1892–1973)*

The most important thing in communication is to hear what isn't being said. —*Peter Drucker (1909-)*

Rank does not confer privilege or give power. It imposes responsibility. —*Peter Drucker (1909-)*

The measure of life, after all, is not its duration, but its donation. —*Peter Marshall (1902–1949)*

This one thing I do, forgetting those things which are behind, and reaching forth unto those things which are before, I press toward the mark! —*Philippians 3:13*

Do not pray for easy lives, pray to be stronger men! Do not pray for tasks equal to your powers, pray for powers equal to your tasks. —*Phillips Brooks (1835–1893)*

No man has come to true greatness who has not felt in some degree that his life belongs to his race, and that what God gives him he gives him for mankind. —*Phillips Brooks (1835–1893)*

Commit to the Lord whatever you do, and your plans will succeed. —*Proverbs 16:3 (NIV)*

Where there is no vision, the people perish. —*Proverbs 29:18*

Our chief want in life is somebody who will make us do what we can.
—*Ralph Waldo Emerson (1803–1882)*

To know even one life has breathed easier because you have lived—this is to have succeeded.
—*Ralph Waldo Emerson (1803–1882)*

Trust the actions and impulses of your soul—venture bravely and all is well.
—*Ralph Waldo Emerson (1803–1882)*

Great men are they who see that spiritual force is stronger than any material force—that thoughts rule the world. —*Ralph Waldo Emerson (1803–1882)*

There are men who by their sympathetic attractions, carry nations with them.
—*Ralph Waldo Emerson (1803–1882)*

Every great and commanding movement in the annals of the world is the triumph of enthusiasm. Nothing great was ever achieved without it. —*Ralph Waldo Emerson (1803–1882)*

Opportunity is a moving target, and the bigger the opportunity, the faster it moves.
—*Richard Gaylord Briley (1930-)*

There is no teaching to compare with example. —*Robert Baden-Powell (1858–1941)*

The difference between possible and impossible is hard work and commitment. —*Robert Dole (1923-)*

The reason why worry kills more people than work is that more people worry than work.
—*Robert Frost (1874–1963)*

The world is full of willing people; some willing to work, the others willing to let them.
—*Robert Frost (1874–1963)*

What great things would you attempt if you knew you could not fail? —*Robert Fuller (1845–1919)*

If you are reasonably sure of your course, just keep on going. —*Robert K. Greenleaf (1904-1990)*

The secret of success is to find the need and fill it, to find a hurt and heal it, to find somebody with a problem and offer to help solve the problem. —*Robert H. Schuller (1926-)*

When you've exhausted all possibilities, remember this: you haven't! —*Robert H. Schuller (1926-)*

Don't kill the dream—execute it! —*Robert H. Schuller (1926-)*

You won't win if you don't begin! —*Robert H. Schuller (1926-)*

For anything new to emerge there must first be a dream, an imaginative view of what might be.
—*Robert K. Greenleaf (1904–1990)*

If at first you don't succeed—try, try again. Don't think of it as failure. Think of it as timed-release success. —*Robert Orben (1927-)*

It's not been so much our resources or our government that have given us our enduring vibrancy and growth, but the initiative and enterprise of individual Americans. —*Ronald Reagan (1911-)*

Pray to God, but keep rowing to the shore. —*Russian Proverb*

No man who is enthusiastic about his work has anything to fear from life.
—*Samuel Goldwyn (1882–1974)*

From success you get a lot of things, but not that great inside thing that love brings you.
—*Samuel Goldwyn (1882–1974)*

Don't look back. . .something may be gaining on you. —*Satchel Paige (1906–1982)*

The sad truth is that excellence makes people nervous. —*Shana Alexander (1925-)*

To do anything in this world worth doing, we must not stand back shivering and thinking of the cold and danger, but jump in, and scramble through as well as we can. —*Sydney Smith (1771–1845)*

Good judgment comes from experience, and experience—well, that comes from poor judgment.
—*Simon Bolivar Buckner (1823–1914)*

We shall steer safely through every storm as long as our heart is right, our intention fervent, our courage steadfast, and our trust fixed on God. —*St. Francis de Sales (1567–1622)*

I am a great believer in luck, and I find the harder I work the more I have of it.
—*Stephen Leacock (1869–1944)*

Failure is impossible. —*Susan B. Anthony (1820–1906)*

Be gentle to all and stern with yourself. —*Teresa of Avila (1515–1582)*

Who escapes a duty, avoids a gain. —*Theodore Parker (1810–1860)*

The rule of brotherhood remains as the indispensable prerequisite to success in the kind of national life for which we strive. —*Theodore Roosevelt (1858–1919)*

Every noble work is at first impossible. —*Thomas Carlyle (1795–1881)*

The reason a lot of people do not recognize opportunity is because it usually goes around wearing overalls looking like hard work. —*Thomas Edison (1847–1931)*

I never did anything worth doing by accident; nor did any of my inventions come by accident; they came by work. —*Thomas Edison (1847–1931)*

I never was much for saving money, as money. I devoted every cent, regardless of future needs, to scientific books and materials for experiments. —*Thomas Edison (1847–1931)*

An idea is something that won't work unless you do. —*Thomas Edison (1847–1931)*

Nothing is so difficult but it may be won by industry. —*Thomas Fuller (1654–1734)*

The great end of life is not knowledge but action. —*Thomas Huxley (1825–1895)*

Now I get me up to work, I pray the Lord I may not shirk, And if I die before tonight, I pray my work will be all right. —*Thomas Osborne Davis (1814–1845)*

I was successful because you believed in me. —*Ulysses S. Grant (1822–1885)*

The reason so few reach the top is because no successful method has yet been devised by which a person may sit down and slide uphill. —*Unknown*

Only through caring and helping can life's true successes be found. —*Unknown*

A diamond is a chunk of coal that made good under pressure. —*Unknown*

To have grown wise and kind is real success. —*Unknown*

A few moments of misplaced values can mean a lifetime of regret. —*Unknown*

When on the ladder of success, don't step back to admire your work. —*Unknown*

Do not follow where the path may lead. Go, instead, where there is no path, and leave a trail.
—*Unknown*

Plan ahead. It wasn't raining when Noah built the ark. —*Unknown*

Good work is seldom an accident. It's done by people who care. —*Unknown*

Dream great dreams and make them come true. —*Unknown*

We are judged by what we finish, not what we start. —*Unknown*

If at first you do succeed—try to hide your astonishment. —*Unknown*

Efficiency is not in doing the unusual well but in doing the usual unusually well. —*Unknown*

Enthusiasm finds the opportunities, and energy makes the most of them. —*Unknown*

We are what we repeatedly do. Excellence, then, is not an act but a habit. —*Unknown*

Hard work is the yeast that raises the dough. —*Unknown*

The Lord gave you two ends—one for sitting and one for thinking. Your success depends on which you use—heads you win, tails you lose. —*Unknown*

Every job is a self-portrait of the person who did it. Autograph your work with excellence! —*Unknown*

The mark of a motivated man is his ability to distinguish a setback from a defeat. —*Unknown*

Every worthwhile accomplishment, big or little, has its stages of drudgery and triumph; a beginning, a struggle, and a victory. —*Unknown*

Success can never be measured by bank balances; money measures only prosperity. Success is a matter of character. —*Unknown*

Success is . . . in the little things you do, and in the things you say. Success is not in getting rich, or rising high to fame. . . . Success is being big of heart, and clean and broad in mind; it's being faithful to your friends, and to the stranger, kind. —*Unknown*

Success lies not in being the best, but in doing your best. —*Unknown*

Success: The proper ratio between what one contributes and what one derives from life. —*Unknown*

Successful folks don't just entertain thoughts — they put them to work. —*Unknown*

Between tomorrow's dream and yesterday's regret is today's opportunity. —*Unknown*

One machine can do the work of fifty ordinary people. No machine can do the work of one extraordinary person. —*Unknown*

Take time to think, it is the source of power. —*Unknown*

When trouble comes, weak men take to the woods; wise men take to their work. —*Unknown*

Do not get mixed up in factions. Keep out of all little bug-house squabbles. Do not take sides—we are here to work, don't you know that? —*Unknown*

The sure way to miss success is to miss the opportunity. —*Victor Chasles (1798–1873)*

It's not whether you get knocked down. It's whether you get up again.
—*Vincent Lombardi (1913–1970)*

Winning is not everything—but making the effort to win is. —*Vincent Lombardi (1913–1970)*

The quality of a person's life is in direct proportion to their commitment to excellence. . . and to victory regardless of what field he may be in. —*Vincent Lombardi (1913–1970)*

What would life be if we had no courage to attempt anything? —*Vincent van Gogh (1853–1890)*

When we are working at a difficult task and strive after a good thing, we are fighting a righteous battle, the direct reward of which is that we are kept from much evil. —*Vincent van Gogh (1853–1890)*

They are able because they think they are able. They can because they think they can.
—*Virgil (70–19 B.C.)*

To make ideas effective, we must be able to fire them off. We must put them into action.
—*Virginia Woolf (1882–1941)*

Success is achieved by those who try and ask. —*W. Clement Stone (1902-)*

Success or failure in business is caused more by mental attitude even than by mental capacities.
—*Walter D. Scott (1869–1955)*

It is a funny thing about life; if you refuse to accept anything but the best, you very often get it.
—*W. Somerset Maugham (1874–1965)*

Out of every fruition of success, no matter what, comes forth something to make a new effort necessary.
—*Walt Whitman (1819–1892)*

Success is not counted by how high you have climbed but by how many you brought with you.
—*Wil Rose (1931-)*

It is fair to judge people and stained-glass windows only in their best light.
—*William Arthur Ward (1921-)*

The price of excellence is discipline. The cost of mediocrity is disappointment.
—*William Arthur Ward (1921-)*

Whatever other gifts you have, if you are to succeed, you must have hearts, and hearts that can feel.
—*William Booth (1829–1912)*

To give life a meaning, one must have a purpose larger than self. —*William Durant (1861–1947)*

Success in business hinges mostly on the ability to get the important things done.
—*William Feather (1870–1944)*

Success seems to be largely a matter of hanging on after others have let go.
—*William Feather (1870–1944)*

In helping others to succeed we insure our own success. —*William Feather (1870–1944)*

The man with the average mentality, but with control; with a definite goal and a clear conception of how it can be gained, and above all, with the power of application and labor, wins in the end.
—*William H. Taft (1857–1930)*

Success is not searching for you. You must do the seeking. Destiny is not a matter of chance, it is a matter of choice; it is not a thing to be waited for, it is a thing to be achieved.
—*William Jennings Bryan (1860–1925)*

The world belongs to the enthusiast who keeps cool. —*William McFee (1881–1966)*

Six essential qualities that are the key to success: sincerity, personal integrity, humility, courtesy, wisdom, charity. —*William Menninger (1899–1966)*

It is no use saying "we are doing our best." You have got to succeed in doing what is necessary. —*Winston Churchill (1874–1965)*

If you mean to profit, learn to please. —*Winston Churchill (1874–1965)*

Success is going from failure to failure without loss of enthusiasm. —*Winston Churchill (1874–1965)*

Success is never final. Failure is never fatal. Courage is the only thing. —*Winston Churchill (1874–1965)*

Those whose work and pleasures are one are fortune's favorite children. —*Winston Churchill (1874–1965)*

The price of greatness is responsibility. —*Winston Churchill (1874–1965)*

Outstanding people have one thing in common: an absolute sense of mission. —*Zig Ziglar (1926-)*

THANKFULNESS
Gratitude • Gratefulness • Appreciation
Acknowledgement • Contentment

In gratitude for your own good fortune you must render in return some sacrifice of your life for another life. —*Albert Schweitzer (1875–1965)*

One can never pay in gratitude; one can only pay in 'kind' somewhere else.
—*Anne Morrow Lindbergh (1906-)*

When you consider everything we have is a gift from God, it's amazing how little gratitude we show. Giving to others is such a small way to say thank you. —*Charles L. Overby (1946-)*

For today and its blessings, I owe the world an attitude of gratitude. —*Clarence E. Hodges (1939-)*

No man who does a good deed should expect gratitude. The reward of a good deed is in having done it.
—*Elbert Hubbard (1856–1915)*

Gratitude is a humble emotion. It expresses itself . . . not for the gifts of this day only, but for the day itself; not for what we believe will be ours in the future, but for the bounty of the past.
—*Faith Baldwin (1893–1978)*

Gratitude to benefactors is a well-recognized virtue, and to express it in some form or other, however imperfectly, is a duty to ourselves as well as to those who have helped us.
—*Frederick Douglass (1817–1895)*

Gratitude is the heart's memory. —*French Proverb*

The ultimate test of man's conscience may be his willingness to sacrifice something today for future generations whose words of thanks will not be heard. —*Gaylord Nelson (1916-)*

One gives praise to God not only through prayers of thanksgiving, but also through obedience to His commandments and service to others, especially those less fortunate than ourselves. —*George Bush (1924-)*

There is nothing that can have a more powerful effect on your mental health than the spirit of thankfulness. —*George E. Vandeman (1916-)*

Swift gratitude is the sweetest. —*Greek Proverb*

So much has been given to me; I have no time to ponder over that which has been denied. —*Helen Keller (1880–1968)*

Thanksgiving is nothing if not a glad and reverent lifting of the heart to God in honor and praise for His goodness. —*James R. Miller (1840–1912)*

Gratitude is a duty which ought to be paid, but which none have a right to expect. —*Jean-Jacques Rousseau (1712–1778)*

He who receives a benefit with gratitude repays the first installment on his debt. —*Lucius Annaeus Seneca (4 B.C.–A.D.65)*

Let the man who would be grateful, think of repaying a kindness, even while receiving it. —*Lucius Annaeus Seneca (4 B.C.–A.D.65)*

There is no quality I would rather have, and be thought to have, than gratitude. For it is not only the greatest virtue, but is the mother of all the rest. —*Marcus Tullius Cicero (106–43 B.C.)*

If you wish your merit to be known, acknowledge that of other people. —*Oriental Proverb*

The worship most acceptable to God comes from a thankful and cheerful heart. —*Plutarch (350–430)*

Every faculty is a gift for the use of which we are responsible to our Creator. —*Proverb*

O give thanks unto the Lord, for he is good: for his mercy endureth for ever. —*Psalms 107:1*

O Lord my God, I will give thanks unto thee for ever. —*Psalms 30:12*

It is a good thing to give thanks to the Lord, and to sing praises to thy name, O most High.
—*Psalms 92:1 (RSV)*

One ungrateful man does an injury to all who stand in need of aid. —*Publius Syrus (c. 1 B.C.)*

A man's indebtedness is not virtue; his repayment is. Virtue begins when he dedicates himself actively to the job of gratitude. —*Ruth Benedict (1887–1948)*

No duty is more urgent than that of returning thanks. —*St. Ambrose (340–397 B.C.)*

In the fabric of gratitude are woven the threads of humility. —*Steven Vitrano (1922-)*

Those who are contented are never poor. —*T. C. Lai (1921-)*

The happiest people are those who are contributing to society. —*Ted Turner (1938-)*

Thanksgiving is the only kind of giving some people know. —*Unknown*

It isn't what you have in your pocket that makes you thankful, but what you have in your heart.
—*Unknown*

A person doesn't know how much he has to be thankful for until he has to pay taxes on it. —*Unknown*

If you can't be content with what you have received, be thankful for what you have escaped. —*Unknown*

Better than thanksgiving is thanksliving. —*Unknown*

If you are really thankful, what do you do? You share. —*W. Clement Stone (1902-)*

Gratitude can transform common days into thanksgiving, turn routine jobs into joy, and change ordinary opportunities into blessings. —*William Arthur Ward (1921-)*

We can no other answer make but thanks, and thanks and ever thanks.
—*William Shakespeare (1564–1616)*

O Lord that lends me life, lend me a heart replete with thankfulness.
—*William Shakespeare (1564–1616)*

VIRTUE

**Beauty • Distinction • Perfection
Character • Excellence**

It is by those only who are truly great, that virtue is esteemed more than riches or honors, or that virtuous actions can be duly appreciated. —*Aldrude (fl. 1170)*

Courage is the price that life exacts for granting peace. —*Amelia Earhart (1898–1937)*

Life shrinks or expands in proportion to one's courage. —*Anais Nin (1903–1977)*

One man with courage makes a majority. —*Andrew Jackson (1767–1845)*

One of the secrets of a long and fruitful life is to forgive everybody everything every night before you go to bed. —*Ann Landers (1918-)*

What is virtue? It is to hold yourself to your fullest development as a person and as a responsible member of the human community. —*Arthur Dobrin (1943-)*

Nothing is so full of victory as patience. He that can have patience, can have what he will.
—*Benjamin Franklin (1706–1790)*

It doesn't matter if you try and try and try again, and fail. It does matter if you try and fail, and fail to try again. —*Charles F. Kettering (1876–1958)*

It's great to be able to pinch your side and find there's not too much fat. Can you pinch your soul and find the same? —*Christopher Blake (1951-)*

Five things constitute perfect virtue: gravity, magnanimity, earnestness, sincerity, kindness.
—*Confucius (551-479 B.C.)*

Worry doesn't empty tomorrow of its sorrow; it empties today of its strength.
—*Corrie Ten Boom (1892–1983)*

Wisdom is knowing what to do next. Virtue is doing it. —*David Starr Jordan (1851–1931)*

Courage is as often the outcome of despair as of hope; in the one case we have nothing to lose, in the other everything to gain. —*Diane de Poitiers (1499–1566)*

The only force that can overcome an idea and a faith is another and better idea and faith, positively and fearlessly upheld. —*Dorothy Thompson (1894–1961)*

No one can make you feel inferior without your consent. —*Eleanor Roosevelt (1884–1962)*

I thank God I am endued with such qualities that if I were turned out of the realm in my petticoat, I were able to live in any place in Christendom. —*Elizabeth I (1533–1603)*

Every man who praises himself brushes the luster from his best efforts. —*Ellen G. White (1827–1915)*

Health is a great treasure. It is the richest possession mortals can have. Wealth, honor, or learning is dearly purchased, if it be at the loss of the vigor of health. None of these attainments can secure happiness, if health is wanting. —*Ellen G. White (1827–1915)*

Everyone has talent. What is rare is the courage to follow the talent to the dark place where it leads.
—*Erica Jong (1943-)*

There is just one virtue—the eternal sacrifice of self. —*George Sand (1804–1876)*

Few men have virtue to withstand the highest bidder. —*George Washington (1732–1799)*

Obstacles are those frightful things you see when you take your eyes off the goal.
—*Hannah Moore (1745–1833)*

True courage consists not in flying from the storms of life, but in braving and steering through them with prudence. —*Hannah Webster Foster (1758–1840)*

I never fight . . . except against difficulties. —*Helen Keller (1880–1968)*

Selfishness is that detestable vice which no one will forgive in others, and no one is without in himself.
—*Henry Ward Beecher (1813–1887)*

To be meek, patient, tactful, modest, honorable, brave, is not to be either manly or womanly; it is to be humane. —*Jane Harrison (1850–1928)*

You can't plant the seed and pick the fruit the next morning. —*Jesse Jackson (1941-)*

So our lives, in acts exemplary, not only win ourselves good names; but doth to others give matter for virtuous deeds by which we live. —*John Chapman "Johnny Appleseed" (1774–1845)*

'Tis virtue, and not birth that makes us noble; great actions speak to great minds.
—*John Fletcher (1579–1625)*

Everyone has special talents, and it is our duty to find ours and use them well.
—*John Templeton (1912-)*

It may seem paradoxical, but if you have some respect for people as they are, you can be more effective in helping them to become better than they are. —*John W. Gardner (1912-)*

All of us celebrate our values in our behavior. —*John W. Gardner (1912-)*

One exemplary act may affect one life, or even millions of lives. All those who set standards for themselves, who strengthen the bonds of community, who do their work creditably and accept individual responsibility are building the common future. —*John W. Gardner (1912-)*

To measure the man measure his heart. —*Malcolm S. Forbes (1919–1990)*

Courage is resistance to fear, mastery of fear, not absence of fear. —*Mark Twain (1835–1910)*

Do something every day that you don't want to do. This is the golden rule for acquiring the habit of doing your duty without pain. —*Mark Twain (1835–1910)*

The ultimate measure of a man is not where he stands in moments of comfort and convenience, but where he stands at times of challenge and controversy. —*Martin Luther King, Jr. (1929–1968)*

Health is not a condition of matter, but of mind; nor can the material senses bear reliable testimony on the subject of health. —*Mary Baker Eddy (1821–1910)*

You can't be brave if you've only had wonderful things happen to you. —*Mary Tyler Moore (1937-)*

Selfishness is the root and source of all natural and moral evils. —*Nathaniel Emmons (1745–1840)*

There's not much you cannot do if you'll give the credit to others. —*Peter M. Buchanan (1935-)*

They that value not praise, will never do anything worthy of it. —*Proverb*

A soft answer turneth away wrath. —*Proverbs 15:1*

Live in harmony with one another. Do not be proud . . . or conceited. —*Romans 12:16 (NIV)*

Never let your head hang down. Never give up and sit down and grieve. Find another way. And don't pray when it rains if you don't pray when the sun shines. —*Satchel Paige (1906–1982)*

True virtue has no limits, but goes on and on, and especially holy charity, which is the virtue of virtues, and which, having an infinite object, would become infinite if it could meet with a heart capable of infinity. —*St. Francis de Sales (1567–1622)*

When a man appears before the Throne of Judgment, the first question he will be asked is not 'have you believed in God' or 'have you prayed and observed the ritual?', but 'have you dealt honorably with your fellow man?' —*The Talmud*

I care not what others think of what I do, but I care very much about what I think of what I do: that is character! —*Theodore Roosevelt (1858–1919)*

He that cannot forgive others breaks the bridge over which he must pass himself; for every man has need to be forgiven. —*Thomas Fuller (1865–1934)*

To forgive heals the wound, to forget heals the scar. —*Unknown*

A good way to forget your troubles is to help others out of theirs. —*Unknown*

What you possess in this world will go to someone else when you die, but what you are will be yours forever. —*Unknown*

You cannot be your brother's keeper if you are caged by selfishness. —*Unknown*

If you do not tell the truth about yourself you cannot tell it about other people. —*Virginia Woolf (1882–1941)*

Every great man, every successful man, no matter what the field of endeavor, has known the magic that lies in these words: every adversity has the seed of an equivalent or greater benefit. —*W. Clement Stone (1902-)*

He who is not liberal with what he has, does not but deceive himself when he thinks he would be liberal if he had more. —*W. S. Plumer (1802–1880)*

We can throw stones, complain about them, stumble on them, climb over them, or build with them. —*William Arthur Ward (1921-)*

A virtuous man will teach himself to recollect the principle of universal benevolence as often as pious men repeat their prayers. —*William Godwin (1756–1836)*

To hoard up all to ourselves is great injustice as well as ingratitude. —*William Penn (1644–1718)*

Difficulties mastered are opportunities won. —*Winston Churchill (1874–1965)*

VOLUNTARISM

Charity • Generosity • Philanthropy
Involvement • Serving

One volunteer is better than ten forced men. —*African Proverb*

To be a good volunteer takes faith and then the willingness to act upon that faith. We must have faith in people, in ourselves, in the spiritual resources that exist in every person.
—*Arthur B. Langlie (1900–1966)*

Volunteering creates a national character in which the community and the nation take on a spirit of compassion, comradeship, and confidence. —*Brian O'Connell (1930-)*

Community partnerships, nonfinancial investments, and profitable social responsibility can offer companies of all sizes new ways to widen their community relationships. And community involvement is definitely good business. —*C. William Verity, Jr. (1917-)*

Individual volunteers are an important basic in the institutional scheme of things. . . . Adequately qualified fund raising volunteers are a precious commodity. —*Edgar D. Powell (1922–1984)*

The act of volunteering is an assertion of individual worth. —*Edward C. Linderman (1885–1953)*

Our United States has become a great nation because its people have engaged — from the earliest years — in voluntarism. They have shown concern for each other in good, as well as bad, times. We must do everything within our power to nurture caring and giving. —*George Bush (1924-)*

The usual trouble with volunteers is not killing them with overwork, but simply boring them to death. —*Harold J. Seymour (1894–1968)*

Causes don't need workers so much as they need informed and dedicated advocates.
—*Harold J. Seymour (1894–1968)*

Every cause needs people more than money, for when the people are with you and are giving your cause their attention, interest, confidence, advocacy and service, financial support should just about take care of itself; whereas, without them in the right quality and quantity in the right places and the right states of mind and spirit, you might as well go and get lost. —*Harold J. Seymour (1894–1968)*

Volunteering can be an exciting, growing, enjoyable experience. It is truly gratifying to serve a cause, practice one's ideals, work with people . . . solve problems. . . , see benefits and know one had a hand in them. —*Harriet Naylor (1915-)*

It is a rare and a high privilege to be in a position to help people understand the difference that they can make not only in their own lives but in the lives of others by simply giving of themselves.
—*Helen Boosalis (1919-)*

One of the characteristics of American society. . . is its reliance on individual initiative and voluntary action to achieve goals. —*Helen Boosalis (1919-)*

The fabric of American life is woven around our tens of thousands of voluntary associations. . .
—*Herbert C. Hoover (1874–1964)*

If you would like to live in a community in which you may have pride, then dedicate yourself in a spirit of humility to your responsibilities in that community. —*Herbert Victor Prochnow (1897-)*

Energy abounds when you volunteer—do it now. —*Holly Stewart McMahon (1953-)*

I feel that the greatest reward for doing is the opportunity to do more. —*Jonas Salk (1914-)*

These are indeed grave times, difficult times, complex times, for your institution. But there have never been more opportunities. And there has never been a more exciting time to be a volunteer for a good cause.
—*Jerold Panas (1928-)*

If there is one word that describes our form of society in America, it may be the word—voluntary.
—*Lyndon B. Johnson (1908–1973)*

Voluntarism is the manifestation of an attitude that breathes selfless activity into certain lives.
—*Mary Lawrence (1953-)*

Voluntarism flourishes in a free society among individuals who live by the Golden Rule, yet see the need for self-actualization. —*Mary Lawrence (1953-)*

Volunteers are an organization's biggest fans and best critics. —*Mary Lawrence (1953-)*

Our country was built on voluntarism, and we need to do all we can to perpetuate this unique quality that has made our nation so great. —*Marilyn Erickson (1928-)*

Caring must strengthen into commitment and commitment into action if we are to preserve and nurture one of the greatest forces for rebirth and renewal this nation has. . . voluntarism.
—*Marlene Wilson (1931-)*

The volunteer has become a major force in our lives . . . because it is not possible for man to live separated from others. We are involved in each others' lives, not by choice but by necessity.
—*Nils Schweizer (1925–1988)*

Volunteer solicitors will gain considerable asking power after they have made gifts of their own.
—*Richard K. Fox (1909-)*

I want to thank and pay tribute to all of our volunteers—those dedicated people who believe in all work and no pay. —*Robert Orben (1927-)*

The genius of the tradition as it has developed in America is the unique combination of giving and voluntary service in behalf of independent organizations and institutions devoted to the public interest.
—*Robert L. Payton (1926-)*

Our American tradition of neighbor helping neighbor has always been one of our greatest strengths and most noble traditions. —*Ronald Reagan (1911-)*

The spirit of voluntarism and compassion for others is a vital part of our national character.
—*Ronald Reagan (1911-)*

The spirit of voluntarism is deeply ingrained in us as a nation . . . . The American people understand that there are no substitutes for gifts of service given from the heart. —*Ronald Reagan (1911-)*

I hope all Americans will vigorously participate in their community's efforts to better the lives of their fellow citizens. —*Ronald Reagan (1911-)*

I'm calling on you today to help in the cause to enlarge the social responsibility of our citizens. The spirit that built this country still dwells in our people. They want to help—we only need to ask them.
—*Ronald Reagan (1911-)*

No matter how big and powerful government gets and the many services it provides, it can never take the place of volunteers. —*Ronald Reagan (1911-)*

We honor the best in every American—that selfless giving spirit of voluntarism which lends a helping hand in brotherhood and neighborliness to those in need. —*Ronald Reagan (1911-)*

Three words take on their true meaning when we see them as verbs more than nouns: volunteer, love, God. —*Sue Vineyard (1938-)*

Others! —*William Booth (1829–1912)*

Nothing but what you volunteer has the essence of life, the springs of pleasure in it. These are the things you do because you want to do them, the things your spirit has chosen for its satisfaction. . . . The more you are stimulated to such action the more clearly does it appear to you that you are a sovereign spirit, put into the world, not to wear a harness, but to work eagerly without it. —*Woodrow Wilson (1856–1924)*

The spirit of voluntarism and generous individual giving must continue to be the special virtue we exhibit. In that spirit will be found life's finest experiences. —*Winfield C. Dunn (1927-)*

WEALTH
Money • Riches • Possessions
Fortune • Luxury

Some people are more turned on by money than they are by love. In one respect they are alike. They're both wonderful as long as they last. —*Abigail Van Buren (1918-)*

This country cannot afford to be materially rich and spiritually poor. —*Abraham Lincoln (1809–1865)*

Silver and gold have I none; but such as I have give I thee. —*Acts 3:6*

Complete possession is proved only by giving. All you are unable to give possesses you.
—*Andre Gide (1869–1951)*

The man who dies leaving behind him millions of available wealth, which was his to administer during life, will pass away "unwept, unhonored, and unsung," no matter to what uses he leaves the dross which he cannot take with him. —*Andrew Carnegie (1835–1919)*

The man who dies rich dies disgraced. —*Andrew Carnegie (1835–1919)*

Surplus wealth is a sacred trust which its possessor is bound to administer in his lifetime for the good of the community. —*Andrew Carnegie (1835–1919)*

The problem of our age is the proper administration of wealth, so that the ties of brotherhood may still bind together the rich and poor in harmonious relationship. —*Andrew Carnegie (1835–1919)*

Too many people today know the price of everything and the value of nothing. —*Ann Landers (1918-)*

Poverty does not mean the possession of little but the nonpossession of much.
—*Antipater (398–319 B.C.)*

If you have great wealth, give alms out of your abundance; if you have but little, distribute even some of that. But do not hesitate to give alms. —*Apocrypha*

Health and good estate of body are above all gold, and a strong body above infinite wealth. —*Apocrypha*

Every man is the architect of his fortune. —*Appius Claudius (c. 321 B.C.)*

The risks of luxury must be balanced against the costs of necessity and proof of utility.
—*Arthur C. Frantzreb (1920-)*

Money is human happiness in the abstract. —*Arthur Schopenhauer (1788–1860)*

Money is like sea water: The more we drink, the thirstier we become.
—*Arthur Schopenhauer (1788–1860)*

Wealth is the product of man's capacity to think. —*Ayn Rand (1905–1982)*

Real riches are the riches possessed inside. —*B. C. Forbes (1880–1954)*

Riches are mental, not material. —*B. C. Forbes (1880–1954)*

Possession hinders enjoyment. It merely gives you the right to keep things from others, and thus you gain more enemies than friends. —*Baltasar Gracian (1601–1658)*

The greatest good you can do for another is not just to share your riches but to reveal to him his own.
—*Benjamin Disraeli (1804–1881)*

Early to bed, early to rise, makes a man healthy, wealthy and wise. —*Benjamin Franklin (1706–1790)*

The use of money is all the advantage there is in having it. —*Benjamin Franklin (1706–1790)*

Who is wise? He that learns from everyone. Who is powerful? He that governs his passions. Who is rich? He that is content. —*Benjamin Franklin (1706–1790)*

If a man empties his purse into his head, no man can take it away from him, for an investment in knowledge pays the best interest. —*Benjamin Franklin (1706–1790)*

It is preoccupation with possessions, more than anything else, that prevents men from living freely and nobly. —*Bertrand Russell (1872–1970)*

Wealth shines in giving rather than in hoarding, for the miser is hated whereas the generous man is applauded. —*Boethius (470-525)*

Both riches and honor come of thee, and thou reignest over all; and in this hand is power and might; and in thine hand it is to make great, and to give strength unto all. —*I Chronicles 29:12*

Moreover it is required in stewards, that a man be found faithful. — *I Corinthians 4:2*

The only things we can keep are the things we freely give to God. What we try to keep for ourselves is just what we are sure to lose. —*C. S. Lewis (1898–1963)*

Wealth, after all, is a relative thing, since he that has little and wants less, is richer than he that has much and wants more. —*Charles Caleb Colton (1780–1832)*

Prosperity is only an instrument to be used, not a deity to be worshiped.
—*Calvin Coolidge (1872–1933)*

We want wealth, but there are many other things we want very much more. Among them are peace, honor, charity, and idealism. —*Calvin Coolidge (1872–1933)*

Money—if it sticks to you, it shrivels you. If you learn to give it away then you open yourself to receive more. —*Carl George (1939-)*

Two things are as big as the man who possesses them, neither bigger nor smaller. One is a minute, the other is a dollar. —*Channing Pollock (1880–1946)*

Economy is half the battle of life; it is not so hard to earn money as to spend it wisely.
—*Charles H. Spurgeon (1834–1892)*

My motto is: Contented with little, yet wishing for more. —*Charles Lamb (1775–1834)*

Let us be known by our deeds, and not by our money. —*Charles Stewart Mott (1875–1973)*

Gold constitutes treasure, and he who possesses it has all the needs in this world, and also the means of rescuing souls. . . . —*Christopher Columbus (1451–1506)*

I have never felt any hesitation in speaking to my congregation about money. I thrill to it. I revel in it. I love to see the liberal enjoy it; I love to watch the stingy suffer. —*Clovis G. Chappell (1882–1972)*

There are people who have money and people who are rich. —*Coco Chanel (1883–1971)*

When wealth is centralized, the people are dispersed. When wealth is distributed, the people are brought together. —*Confucius (551–479 B.C.)*

It is true that money attracts, but much money repels. —*Cynthia Ozick (1928-)*

Only when the money we earn is put to work for the benefit of others does it provide true satisfaction. —*D. Malcolm Maxwell (1934-)*

All good things of this world are no further good than as they are of use; and whatever we may heap up to give others, we enjoy only as much as we can make useful to ourselves and others, and no more. —*Daniel Defoe (1661–1731)*

No one is rich enough to do without a neighbor. —*Danish Proverb*

Remember that it is the Lord your God who gives you the power to become rich. —*Deuteronomy 8:18 (TEV)*

Money answereth all things. —*Ecclesiastes 10:19*

He that loveth silver shall not be satisfied with silver; nor he that loveth abundance with increase: this is also vanity. —*Ecclesiastes 5:10*

There is a sore evil which I have seen under the sun, namely, riches kept for the owners thereof to their hurt. —*Ecclesiastes 5:13*

Every man also to whom God hath given riches and wealth, and hath given him power to eat thereof, and to take his portion, and to rejoice in his labor; this is the gift of God. —*Ecclesiastes 5:19*

Money would be more enjoyable if it took people as long to spend it as it does to earn it. —*Edgar Watson Howe (1853–1937)*

Men are rich only as they give. He who gives great service gets great returns. —*Elbert Hubbard (1856–1915)*

So-called rich men are simply trustees. All that they have at best is a life-lease on the property. —*Elbert Hubbard (1856–1915)*

The more money you have, the more responsibility you have. —*Eleanor W. Libby (1909-)*

Money is of no value till 'tis used. —*Elizabeth Cooper (fl. 1737-)*

Money is a good servant but a bad master. —*Francis Bacon (1561–1626)*

Money is like muck—not good unless it be spread. —*Francis Bacon (1561–1626)*

The hopes of the Republic cannot forever tolerate either undeserved poverty or self-serving wealth. —*Franklin D. Roosevelt (1882–1945)*

The golden age only comes to men when they have forgotten gold. —*G. K. Chesterton (1874–1936)*

We have no more right to consume happiness without producing it than to consume wealth without producing it. —*George Bernard Shaw (1856–1950)*

Poverty robs one of the right to be generous. —*George Gissing (1857–1903)*

It's good to have money and the things that money can buy. But it's good, too, to check up once in a while and make sure you haven't lost the things money can't buy. —*George Horace Lorimer (1868–1937)*

But for money and the need of it, there would not be half the friendship in the world. It is powerful for good if divinely used. Give it plenty of air and it is as sweet as the hawthorn; shut it up and it cankers and breeds worms. —*George MacDonald (1824–1905)*

It is not a custom with me to keep money to look at. —*George Washington (1732–1799)*

Money is always there but the pockets change. —*Gertrude Stein (1874–1946)*

With luck and resolution and good guidance . . . the human mind can survive not only poverty, but even wealth. —*Gilbert Highet (1906-)*

It's more rewarding to watch money change the world than watch it accumulate. —*Gloria Steinem (1934-)*

Money frees you from doing things you dislike. Since I dislike doing nearly everything, money is handy. —*Groucho Marx (1890–1977)*

Money as money is nothing. —*H. L. Hunt (1889–1974)*

Money is just something to make bookkeeping convenient. —*H. L. Hunt (1889–1974)*

Money does the most good if you do something preventive, rather than something remedial. —*Harriett Stimson Bullitt (1925-)*

Money. . . is a person's personal energy reduced to portable form. . . . It can go where he could not go; speak languages he could not speak; lift burdens he could not touch with his fingers; save lives with which he cannot deal directly. —*Harry Emerson Fosdick (1878–1969)*

One who thinks that money can do everything is likely to do anything for money. —*Hasidic Proverb*

Money may be the husk of many things, but not the kernel. It brings you food, but not appetite; medicine, but not health; acquaintances, but not friends; servants, but not faithfulness; days of joy, but not peace or happiness. —*Henrik Ibsen (1828–1906)*

A man is rich in proportion to the things he can afford to let alone.
—*Henry David Thoreau (1817–1862)*

The man is richest whose pleasures are the cheapest. —*Henry David Thoreau (1817–1862)*

Superfluous wealth can buy superfluities only. Money is not required to buy one necessity of the soul.
—*Henry David Thoreau (1817–1862)*

Make money your God, and it will plague you like the devil. —*Henry Fielding (1707–1754)*

The highest use of capital is not to make more money, but to make money do more for the betterment of life. —*Henry Ford (1863–1947)*

Our money is most truly ours when it ceases to be in our possession. —*Henry Mackenzie (1745–1831)*

Riches are not an end of life but an instrument of life. —*Henry Ward Beecher (1813–1887)*

No man can tell whether he is rich or poor by turning to his ledger. It is the heart that makes a man rich. He is rich or poor according to what he is, not according to what he has.
—*Henry Ward Beecher (1813–1887)*

If money is all that a man makes, then he will be poor—poor in happiness, poor in all that makes life worth living. —*Herbert N. Casson (1869– ?)*

Those who give have all things; those who withhold have nothing. —*Hindu Proverb*

In all abundance there is lack. —*Hippocrates (460–377 B.C.)*

Riches either serve or govern the possessor. —*Horace (65–8 B.C.)*

He will always be a slave who does not know how to live upon a little. —*Horace (65–8 B.C.)*

To make money immortal, invest it in men. —*Horace Mann (1796–1859)*

Money swore an oath that nobody who did not love it should ever have it. —*Irish Proverb*

You shall be fed with the treasures of the nations and shall glory in their riches. Instead of shame and dishonor, you shall have a double portion of prosperity and everlasting joy. —*Isaiah 61:6-7*

He who has money finds many cousins. —*Italian Proverb*

The measure of a man's value is the degree to which he has made a difference in the lives of those he has touched. —*Jackie A. Strange (1927-)*

The surplus wealth we have gained to some extent belongs to our fellow beings; we are only the temporary custodians of our fortunes, and let us be careful that no just complaint can be made against our stewardship. —*Jacob H. Schiff (1847–1920)*

A man's treatment of money is the most decisive test of his character—how he makes it and how he spends it. —*James Moffatt (1870–1944)*

Don't tell me where your priorities are. Show me where you spend your money and I'll tell you what they are. —*James W. Frick (1924-)*

Getting money is like digging with a needle; spending it is like water soaking into sand. —*Japanese Proverb*

You don't seem to realize that a poor person who is unhappy is in a better position than a rich person who is unhappy. Because the poor person has hope. He thinks money would help. —*Jean Kerr (1923-)*

Thus saith the Lord, "Let not the wise man glory in his wisdom, neither let the mighty man glory in his might, let not the rich man glory in his riches." —*Jeremiah 9:23 (NIV)*

When we come into this life, we don't really own anything. And we own nothing when we leave. It is only a lease we have during our lifetime—and it is up to us to make the most of it. —*Jerold Panas (1928-)*

If you have some money, share it. And if you have some time, do something worthwhile. —*Jerome Stone (1913-)*

The rich man carries God in his pocket, the poor man—in his heart. —*Jewish Proverb*

With money in your pocket, you are wise, and you are handsome, and you sing well too. —*Jewish Proverb*

Sad is the man who has nothing but money. —*Jewish Proverb*

I don't like money, actually, but it quiets my nerves. —*Joe Lewis (1914–1981)*

I've been rich and I've been poor, and believe me, rich is better. —*Joe Lewis (1914–1981)*

As I study wealthy men, I can see but one way in which they can secure a real equivalent for money spent, and that is to cultivate a taste for giving where the money may produce an effect which will be a lasting gratification. . . . —*John D. Rockefeller (1839–1937)*

I believe that the power to make money is a gift from God . . . to be developed and used to the best of your ability for the good of mankind. Having been endowed with the gift I possess, I believe it is my duty to make money and still more money, and to use the money I make for the good of my fellow man according to the dictates of my conscience. —*John D. Rockefeller (1839–1937)*

The only question with wealth is what you do with it. —*John D. Rockefeller, Jr. (1874–1960)*

Large was his wealth, but larger was his heart. —*John Dryden (1631–1700)*

If a free society cannot help the many who are poor, it cannot save the few who are rich.
—*John F. Kennedy (1917–1963)*

Wealth is a means to an end, not the end itself. As a synonym for health and happiness, it has had a fair trial and failed dismally. —*John Galsworthy (1867–1933)*

Wealth is not without its advantages and the case to the contrary, although it has often been made, has never proved widely persuasive. —*John Kenneth Galbraith (1908–)*

It is physically impossible for a well-educated, intellectual, or brave man to make money the chief object of his thoughts. —*John Ruskin (1819–1900)*

There is no wealth but life. —*John Ruskin (1819–1900)*

When I have any money I get rid of it as quickly as possible, lest it find a way into my heart.
—*John Wesley (1703–1791)*

A wise man ought to have money in his head, but not in his heart. —*Jonathan Swift (1667–1745)*

Nothing is so hard for those who abound in riches as to conceive how others can be in want.
—*Jonathan Swift (1667–1745)*

The best condition in life is not to be so rich as to be envied nor so poor as to be damned.
—*Josh Billings (1818–1885)*

Money is like love; it kills slowly and painfully the one who withholds it, and it enlivens the other who turns it upon his fellow man. —*Kahlil Gibran (1883–1931)*

The wealthy man is the man who is much, not the one who has much. —*Karl Marx (1818–1883)*

It is fun to have money only if it can help others, but distributing money in a way that makes a difference is a difficult and wonderful challenge. —*Kenneth N. Dayton (1922-)*

Money has little value to its possessor unless it also has value to others.
—*Leland Stanford (1824–1893)*

Money is the root of all excellence. —*Louis E. Bejarano (1917-)*

Once you have money, you can quite truthfully affirm that money isn't everything.
—*Louis Kronenberger (1904–1980)*

For many men, the acquisition of wealth does not end their troubles, it only changes them.
—*Lucius Annaeus Seneca (4 B.C.– A.D. 65)*

Sell what you have and give to those in need. This will fatten your purse in heaven! And the purses of heaven have no rips or holes in them. Your treasures there will never disappear; no thief can steal them; no moth can destroy them. —*Luke 12:33 (LB)*

Where your treasure is, there will your heart be also. —*Luke 12:34*

We are rich only through what we give; and poor only through what we refuse and keep.
—*Anne Swetchine (1782–1857)*

Capital as such is not evil; it is its wrong use that is evil. —*Mahatma Gandhi (1869–1948)*

I am not against wealth; I am against wealth that enslaves. —*Mahatma Gandhi (1869–1948)*

Money is what you'd get on beautifully without if only other people weren't so crazy about it.
—*Margaret Case Harriman (1904–1966)*

What I know about money, I learned the hard way—by having it. —*Margaret Halsey (1910-)*

Being rich, we thought it our duty to hand out a little to the poor around us.
—*Margaret Morris (1737–1816)*

It is not the creation of wealth that is wrong but love of money for its own sake. The spiritual dimension comes in deciding what one does with the wealth. —*Margaret Thatcher (1925-)*

No one would remember the Good Samaritan if he only had good intentions. He had money as well. —*Margaret Thatcher (1925-)*

To be satisfied with what one has; that is wealth. As long as one sorely needs a certain additional amount, that man isn't rich. —*Mark Twain (1835–1910)*

When I was brought up we never talked about money because there was never enough to furnish a topic of conversation. —*Mark Twain (1835–1910)*

Few of us can stand prosperity. Another man's, I mean. —*Mark Twain (1835–1910)*

The richest man in the world is not the one who still has the first dollar he ever earned. It's the man who still has his first friend. —*Martha Mason (1864–1949)*

Lay not up for yourselves treasures upon earth, where moth and rust doth corrupt, and where thieves break through and steal. —*Matthew 6:19*

We are all of us richer than we think we are. —*Michel de Montaigne (1533–1592)*

A man's true wealth is the good he does in this world. —*Mohammed (570–632)*

Riches are not from an abundance of worldly goods, but from a contented mind. —*Mohammed (570–632)*

You can't take it with you. —*Moss Hart & George S. Kaufman*

Riches do not consist in the possession of treasures, but in the use made of them. —*Napoleon Bonaparte (1769–1821)*

He who lives content with little possesses everything. —*Nicolas Boileau (1636–1711)*

No nation became great by becoming rich. Neither does a man find enduring satisfaction in life by owning something—only by becoming something. —*Norman Vincent Peale (1898–1993)*

It's better to have a rich soul than to be rich. —*Olga Korbut (1955-)*

Put not your trust in money, put your money in trust. —*Oliver Wendell Holmes (1809–1894)*

My main philosophy is that my money is a loan from God. I'm in charge of it. I'm responsible for investing it, giving some of it away, providing for my family and protecting it. —*Orel Hershiser, IV (1958-)*

Money cannot bring you happiness, but at least you can be miserable in comfort.
—*Oscar Wilde (1854-1900)*

Money is a terrible master but an excellent servant. —*P. T. Barnum (1810–1891)*

Wealth does not bring excellence, but that wealth comes from excellence. —*Plato (427–347 B.C.)*

By all means get money, not to hoard, but to spend—to procure employment, liberty, independence, and above all, the power of doing good. —*Proverb*

The richest man on earth is but a pauper fed and clothed by the bounty of heaven. —*Proverb*

Riches have made more men covetous, than covetousness hath made men rich. —*Proverb*

Riches well-got, and well-used, are a great blessing. —*Proverb*

If money be not thy servant, it will be thy master. —*Proverb*

He has riches enough who needs neither to borrow nor flatter. —*Proverb*

Of all the dust thrown in men's eyes, gold dust is the most blinding. —*Proverb*

Take care of the pence, the pounds will take care of themselves. —*Proverb*

One man gives freely, yet grows all the richer; another withholds what he should give, and only suffers want. —*Proverbs 11:24*

He that trusteth in his riches shall fall: but the righteous shall flourish as a branch. —*Proverbs 11:28*

Wealth gotten by vanity shall be diminished: but he that gathereth by labor shall increase.
—*Proverbs 13:11*

Some rich people are poor, and some poor people have great wealth! —*Proverbs 13:7 (LB)*

Wealth maketh many friends. —*Proverbs 19:4*

A good name is more desirable than great riches. —*Proverbs 22:1 (NIV)*

The rich and the poor are alike before the Lord who made them all. —*Proverbs 22:2 (LB)*

Better is the poor that walketh in his uprightness, than he that is perverse in his ways, though he be rich. —*Proverbs 28:6*

Give me neither poverty nor riches! Give me just enough to satisfy my needs! —*Proverbs 30:8 (LB)*

I will sing unto the Lord, because He hath dealt bountifully with me. —*Psalms 13:6*

He heapeth up riches, and knoweth not who shall gather them. —*Psalms 39:6*

Blessed be the Lord, who daily loadeth us with benefits, even the God of our salvation. —*Psalms 68:19*

I have rejoiced in the way of thy testimonies, as much as in all riches. —*Psalms 119:14*

Money alone sets all the world in motion. —*Publius Syrus (c. 1 B.C.)*

The greatest man in history was the poorest. —*Ralph Waldo Emerson (1803–1882)*

Get to know two things about a man—how he earns his money and how he spends it—and you have the clue to his character. You will know all you need to know about his standards, his motives, his driving desires and his real religion. —*Robert J. McCracken (1904–1973)*

We are temporary stewards with an obligation to manage the inheritance in such a way that it can be passed along even better and stronger than it was when we received it. —*Robert L. Payton (1926-)*

To seek to improve the lives of others or to work for the common good is to act with moral consequences. —*Robert L. Payton (1926-)*

More people should learn to tell their dollars where to go instead of asking them where they went. —*Roger Babson (1875–1967)*

Money spent on myself may be a millstone about my neck; money spent on others may give me wings like the angels. —*Roswell Dwight Hitchcock (1817–1887)*

For a man to say, 'I do not want money,' is to say, 'I do not wish to do any good to my fellow men.' —*Russell H. Conwell (1843–1925)*

The poor have us always with them. —*Saki (1870–1916)*

A penny will hide the biggest star in the universe if you hold it close enough to your eye. —*Samuel Grafton (1907-)*

Money and time are the heaviest burdens of life and the unhappiest of all mortals are those who have more of either of these than they know how to use. —*Samuel Johnson (1709–1784)*

It is by spending oneself that one becomes rich. —*Sarah Bernhardt (1844–1923)*

The secret of living is to find people who will pay you money to do what you would pay to do if you had the money. —*Sarah Caldwell (1924-)*

Money alone cannot build character or transform evil into good. . . . It cries for full partnership with leaders of character and good will who value good tools in the creation and enlargement of life for Man. . . . —*Sebastian S. Kresge (1867–1966)*

If a rich man is proud of his wealth, he should not be praised until it is known how he employs it. —*Socrates (470–399 B.C.)*

My belief is that to have no wants is divine. —*Socrates (470–399 B.C.)*

Riches are not forbidden, but the pride of them is. —*St. John Chrysostom (345–407)*

The only permanent thing that money can buy is a happy memory. —*Sydney J. Harris (1917-)*

The love of money is the root of all evil. —*I Timothy 6:10*

Do you want to be truly rich? You are already if you are happy and good. —*I Timothy 6:6 (LB)*

As for the rich in this world. . .they are to be rich in good deeds. . .and generous so that they may take hold of the life which is life indeed. —*I Timothy 6:7-10 (RSV)*

Whenever the opportunity comes to give, which is pretty often, we are likely . . . to think of our poverty instead of our wealth. —*T. T. Frankenberg (1877–1958)*

When money is your god, you are never going to be fulfilled, you are never going to be happy, because no matter how much you have, it is not enough. —*Ted Turner (1938-)*

There seem to me a great many blessings which come from true poverty and I should be sorry to be deprived of them. —*Teresa of Avila (1515–1582)*

Wealth and want equally harden the human heart. —*Theodore Parker (1810–1860)*

It is not what we have that will make us a great nation; it is the way in which we use it. —*Theodore Roosevelt (1858–1919)*

The glow of one warm thought is to me worth more than money. —*Thomas Jefferson (1743–1826)*

Taxation, like a lot of other things, is based on supply and demand. The government demands, and we supply. —*Unknown*

Taxes are just like golf—you drive your heart out to get to the green and then end up in the hole. —*Unknown*

The most important things in life aren't things. —*Unknown*

Love of the right use of money is the root of much good. —*Unknown*

May avarice lose his purse and benevolence find it. —*Unknown*

When wealth is lost, nothing is lost;
When health is lost, something is lost;
When character is lost, all is lost.
—*Unknown*

A man never gets so rich he can afford to lose a friend. —*Unknown*

Dollars and sense should go together. —*Unknown*

He is no fool who gives that which he cannot keep in order to gain that which he cannot lose. —*Unknown*

Money talks, but it rarely gives itself away. —*Unknown*

You can't take your money to heaven, but you can invest it for eternity. —*Unknown*

The love of money is the disease which makes men most groveling and pitiful. —*Unknown*

The money you refuse to worthy objects will never do you any good. —*Unknown*

The most important things in life are free, but the second best are expensive. —*Unknown*

Fortune does not so much change men as it unmasks them. —*Unknown*

Everybody shuns trouble unless it comes to him disguised as money. —*Unknown*

A rich man is nothing but a poor man with money. —*W. C. Fields (1879–1946)*

I found that money was like a sixth sense without which you could not make the most of the other five. —*W. Somerset Maugham (1874–1965)*

Personally choosing to have time over having money makes giving more enjoyable. —*William C. McGinly (1946-)*

Money is better than poverty, if only for financial reasons. —*Woody Allen (1935-)*

MISCELLANEOUS
**Peace • Self-Esteem • Time • Nature
Conservation • Imagination**

I pledge my head to clearer thinking, my heart to greater loyalty, my hands to larger service, and my health to better living, for my club, my community, my country and my world. —*4-H Pledge*

The debt that each generation owes to the past it must pay to the future.
—*Abigail Scott Duniway (1834–1915)*

The best index to a person's character is (a) how he treats people who can't do him any good, and (b) how he treats people who can't fight back. —*Abigail Van Buren (1918-)*

All that I am or hope to be I owe to my angel mother. —*Abraham Lincoln (1809–1865)*

Every man is said to have his peculiar ambition. . . . I have no other so great as that of being truly esteemed of my fellow men, by rendering myself worthy of their esteem.
—*Abraham Lincoln (1809–1865)*

Ballots are the rightful and peaceful successors of bullets. —*Abraham Lincoln (1809–1865)*

We abuse the land because we regard it as a commodity belonging to us. When we see land as a community to which we belong, we may begin to use it with love and respect.
—*Aldo Leopold (1886–1948)*

Let us be of good cheer, remembering that the misfortunes hardest to bear are those which never come.
—*Amy Lowell (1874–1925)*

We don't see things as they are, we see them as we are. —*Anais Nin (1903–1977)*

Parents can only give good advice or put [their children] on the right paths, but the final forming of a person's character lies in their own hands. —*Anne Frank (1929–1945)*

The tongue is like a sharp knife: it kills without drawing blood. —*Anne Sexton (1928–1974)*

I have the feeling that in a balanced life one should die penniless. The trick is dismantling. —*Art Garfunkel (1941-)*

In stepping outside of the self and working for the common good, a solidarity with others is confirmed. —*Arthur Dobrin (1943-)*

The deepest personal defeat suffered by human beings is constituted by the difference between what one was capable of becoming, and what one has in fact become. —*Ashley Montagu (1905-)*

Men who are governed by reason . . . desire for themselves nothing which they do not also desire for the rest of mankind. —*Benedict Spinoza (1632–1677)*

A man wrapped up in himself makes a very small bundle. —*Benjamin Franklin (1706–1790)*

But more than all I pray that down the years we will remember there are always new frontiers. —*Birdsell Otis Edey (1872–1940)*

There's nothing so rewarding as to make people realize they are worthwhile in this world. —*Bob Anderson (1917-)*

I resolved that because I had no ancestry myself, I would leave a record of which my children would be proud, and which might encourage them to still higher effort. —*Booker T. Washington (1856–1915)*

There are two ways of exerting one's strength; one is pushing down, the other is pulling up. —*Booker T. Washington (1856–1915)*

A proud man is always looking down on things and people: and, of course, as long as you are looking down, you cannot see something that is above you. —*C. S. Lewis (1898–1963)*

A blunder at the right moment is better than cleverness at the wrong time. —*Carolyn Wells (1870–1942)*

Every dogma must have its day. —*Carolyn Wells (1870–1942)*

My interest is in the future because I'm going to spend the rest of my life there. —*Charles F. Kettering (1876–1958)*

He who deliberates fully before taking a step will spend his entire life on one leg. —*Chinese Proverb*

Since everything is in our heads, we had better not lose them. —*Coco Chanel (1883–1971)*

We are so busy doing the urgent that we don't have time to do the important.
—*Confucius (551–479 B.C.)*

Blessed is he who expects nothing, for he is never disappointed. —*Confucius (551–479 B.C.)*

A mother is not a person to lean on, but a person to make leaning unnecessary.
—*Dorothy Canfield Fisher (1879–1958)*

To look up and not down,
To look forward and not back,
To look out and not in; and
To lend a hand.
—*Edward Everett Hale (1822–1909)*

We have committed the Golden Rule to memory; let us now commit it to life.
—*Edwin Markham (1852–1940)*

It is not fair to ask of others what you are not willing to do yourself. —*Eleanor Roosevelt (1884–1962)*

You are a great person as long as you are the factor that keeps the community doing the right thing.
—*Eleanor Roosevelt (1884–1962)*

For it isn't enough to talk about peace. One must believe in it. And it isn't enough to believe in it. One must
work at it. —*Eleanor Roosevelt (1884–1962)*

When people say. 'She's got everything,' I've only one answer, 'I haven't had tomorrow.'
—*Elizabeth Taylor (1932-)*

The most difficult sermon to preach and the hardest to practice is self-denial.
—*Ellen G. White (1827–1915)*

We should strive to understand the weakness of others. —*Ellen G. White (1827–1915)*

Here lies a good fellow who spent his life while he had it. —*Epitaph of Horatio Alger, Jr. (1834–1899)*

Man is born broken. He lives by mending. And, the grace of God is the glue.
—*Eugene O'Neill (1888–1953)*

We discovered that peace at any price is no peace at all . . . life at any price has no value whatever; . . . life is nothing without the privileges, the prides, the rights, the joys that make it worth living, and also worth giving. —*Eve Curie (1904-)*

I never lose an opportunity of urging a practical beginning, however small, for it is wonderful how often in such matters the mustard-seed germinates and roots itself. —*Florence Nightingale (1820–1910)*

Lord, make me an instrument of thy peace. Where there is hatred, let me now love. Where there is lying, pardon. Where there is doubt, faith. Where there is despair, hope. Where there is darkness, light. Where there is sadness, joy. Oh, Divine Master, grant that I may not so much seek to be consoled as to console, to be understood as to understand, to be loved as to love for it is by giving that we receive, it is in pardoning that we are pardoned, and it is in dying that we are born to eternal life. —St. *Francis of Assisi (1182–1226)*

I don't want to own anything that won't fit into my coffin. —*Fred Allen (1894–1956)*

Each of us comes into life with fists closed, set for aggressiveness and acquisition. But when we abandon life our hands are open; there is nothing on earth that we need, nothing the soul can take with it. —*Fulton J. Sheen (1895–1979)*

In uplifting, get underneath. —*George Ade (1866–1944)*

Some men see things as they are and say 'why?' I dream things that never were, and say, 'why not?' —*George Bernard Shaw (1856–1950)*

Mothers work, not upon canvas that shall perish, nor marble that crumbles into dust, but upon mind, upon spirit, which is to last forever, and which is to bear, for good or evil, throughout its duration, the impress of a mother's plastic hand. —*George Washington (1732–1799)*

Labor to keep alive in your breast that little spark of celestial fire called conscience. —*George Washington (1732–1799)*

Observe good faith and justice toward all nations; cultivate peace and harmony with all. —*George Washington (1732–1799)*

We fought hard. We gave it our best. We did what was right. And we made a difference. —*Geraldine Ferraro (1935-)*

The sense of this word among the Greeks affords the noblest definition of it; enthusiasm signifies "God in us." —*Germaine de Stael (1766–1817)*

The conservation of natural resources is the key to the future. . . . The very existence of our nation, and all the rest, depends on conserving the resources which; are the foundation of its life.
—*Gifford Pinchot (1865–1946)*

Those who don't know how to weep with their whole heart don't know how to laugh either.
—*Golda Meir (1898–1979)*

It is brave to be involved, to be fearful is to be unresolved. —*Gwendolyn Brooks (1917-)*

You get the best out of others when you give the best of yourself.
—*Harvey Firestone (1898–1973)*

Bless us our Father, together all of us, with the light of thy countenance. —*Hebrew Daily Prayer Book*

The best and most beautiful things in the world cannot be seen or even touched. They must be felt with the heart. —*Helen Keller (1880–1968)*

I thank God for my handicaps, for through them I have found myself, my work, and my God.
—*Helen Keller (1880–1968)*

Time is not measured by the years that we live,
But by the deeds that we do and the joys that we give.
—*Helen Steiner Rice (1900–1981)*

We must go out and re-ally ourselves to nature every day. We must take root, send out some little fibre at least, even every winter day. —*Henry David Thoreau (1817–1862)*

To affect the quality of the day—that is the highest use of the arts.
—*Henry David Thoreau (1817–1862)*

No society of nations, no people within a nation, no family can benefit through mutual aid unless good will exceeds ill will; unless the spirit of cooperation surpasses antagonism; unless we all see and act as though the other man's welfare determines our own welfare. —*Henry Ford II (1917–1987)*

Ideas are, in truth, forces. Infinite, too, is the power of personality. A union of the two always makes history. —*Henry James (1843–1916)*

Use what talents you possess: the woods would be very silent if no birds sang there except those that sang best. —*Henry Van Dyke (1852–1933)*

The truest self-respect is not to think of self. —*Henry Ward Beecher (1813–1887)*

Peace is not made at the council table or by treaties, but in the hearts of men. —*Herbert C. Hoover (1874–1964)*

Blessed are the young, for they shall inherit the national debt. —*Herbert C. Hoover (1874–1964)*

My poor are my best patients. God pays for them. —*Hermann Boerhaave (1668–1738)*

Your own property is at stake when your neighbor's house is on fire. —*Horace (65–8 B.C.)*

We could not retard that great forward movement of humanity if we would. But each of us may decide for himself whether to share in the glory of promoting it or incur the shame of having looked coldly and indifferently on. —*Horace Greeley (1812–1872)*

Peace we want because there is another war to fight; against poverty and disease. —*Indira Gandhi (1917–1984)*

Imagination has always had powers of resurrection that no science can match. —*Ingrid Bengis*

I ought, therefore I can. —*Immanuel Kant (1724–1804)*

The shadows will always be behind those who walk toward the light. —*James F. Oates, Jr. (1899–)*

What we really are matters more than what other people think of us. —*Jawaharlal Nehru (1889–1964)*

Pay no attention to what the critics say. A statue has never been created in honor of a critic. —*Jean Sibelius (1865–1957)*

For the aging, the future is today. —*Jerry D. Smart (1935–)*

Shrouds have no pockets. —*Jewish Proverb*

Treat people as if they were what they ought to be and you help them become what they are capable of being. —*Johann Wolfgang von Goethe (1749–1832)*

Nothing is worth more than this day. —*Johann Wolfgang von Goethe (1749–1832)*

I have told you these things, so that in me you may have peace. In this world you will have trouble. But take heart! I have overcome the world. —*John 16:33 (NIV)*

We can pay our debt to the past by putting the future in debt to ourselves.
—*Sir John Buchan (1875–1940)*

Some people strengthen the society just by being the kind of people they are.
—*John W. Gardner (1912-)*

Nature does not demand that we be perfect. It requires only that we grow. —*Josh Liebman (1907–1948)*

Treat the earth well. It was not given to you by your parents. . . . It is loaned to you by your children.
—*Kenyan Proverb*

Children are likely to live up to what you believe of them. —*Lady Bird Johnson (1912-)*

Self-esteem soars in direct proportion to our forgetting the 'self' part.
—*Lady Elleen Hartley-Wigginton (1942-)*

The most practical things in the world are common sense and common humanity.
—*Lady Nancy Astor (1879–1964)*

Collectively we can do what no person can do singly. —*Leland Kaiser (1936-)*

The future is simply infinite possibility waiting to happen. What it waits on is human imagination to crystallize its possibility. —*Leland Kaiser (1936-)*

If the world seems cold to you, kindle fires to warm it. —*Lucy Larcom (1826–1893)*

The wonder of nature is the treasure of America . . . .The precious legacy of preservation of beauty will be our gift to posterity. —*Lyndon B. Johnson (1908–1973)*

We have developed a life-style that is draining the earth, without regard for the future of our children and people all around the world. —*Margaret Mead (1901–1978)*

You really have to look inside yourself and find your own inner strength, and say, "I'm proud of what I am and who I am, and I'm just going to be myself." —*Mariah Carey (1969-)*

The arm of the moral universe is long, but it bends toward justice.
—*Martin Luther King, Jr. (1929–1968)*

To those leaning on the sustaining infinite, today is big with blessings.
—*Mary Baker Eddy (1821–1910)*

It is the creative potential itself in human beings that is the image of God. —*Mary Daly (1928-)*

God does not work in all hearts alike, but according to the preparation and sensitivity He finds in each.
—*Meister Eckhart (1260–1327)*

It is the link from the present to the past that gives us a spirit to address the future.
—*Midge Costanza (1928-)*

There are only two families in the world, the haves and the have-nots.
—*Miguel de Cervantes (1547–1616)*

The idea of strictly minding our own business is moldy rubbish. Who could be so selfish?
—*Myrtie Lillian Barker (1910-)*

People can be divided into three groups: those who make things happen, those who watch things happen, and those who wonder what happened. —*Nicholas Murray Butler (1862–1947)*

We enjoy or suffer the consequences of our ideas, our acts or our hopes, and our fears. . . . I cannot affirm God if I fail to affirm man. —*Norman Cousins (1912-)*

You only lose energy when life becomes dull in your mind. You don't have to be tired and bored. Get interested in something. Get absolutely enthralled in something. Throw yourself into it with abandon.
—*Norman Vincent Peale (1898–1993)*

Imagination is the true magic carpet. —*Norman Vincent Peale (1898–1993)*

The Lord bless you and keep you: the Lord make his face shine upon you, and be gracious to you: the Lord lift up His countenance upon you, and give you peace. —*Numbers 6:24-26 (RSV)*

Think well of yourself and proclaim this fact to the world—not in loud words, but in great deeds.
—*Optimist's Creed*

We're all in the gutter, but some of us are looking at the stars. —*Oscar Wilde (1854–1900)*

Today is unique. Don't let its wonderful moments go by unnoticed and unused. —*Pat Boone (1934-)*

It is impossible to be the best we can be in isolation. —*Paula P. Brownlee (1934-)*

You need circles of community to sustain your continual growth . . . and they must be of your choosing and your building. —*Paula P. Brownlee (1934-)*

Canada is not a country for the cold of heart or the cold of feet. —*Pierre Elliott Trudeau (1919-)*

All the people of a country have a direct interest in conservation. . . . Wildlife, water, forests, grasslands— all are a part of man's essential environment; the conservation and effective use of one is impossible except as the others are also conserved. —*Rachel Carson (1907–1964)*

Reverence for nature is compatible with willingness to accept responsibility for a creative stewardship of the earth. —*René Dubos (1901-)*

What lies behind us and what lies before us are tiny matters compared to what lies within us.
—*Ralph Waldo Emerson (1803–1882)*

Where peace is unknown, make it welcome.
Where peace is fragile, make it strong.
Where peace is temporary, make it permanent.
—*Richard Nixon (1913-)*

A man's reach should exceed his grasp, or what is heaven for? —*Robert Browning (1812–1889)*

It is difficult to say what is impossible, for the dreams of yesterday are the hopes of today, and the realities of tomorrow. —*Robert H. Goddard (1882–1945)*

Self-discipline motivated by concern for others; this has been the standard of conduct which I have attempted to reach. —*Roger Barnes (1897–1982)*

If we are to be responsible, we must accept the fact that we owe a massive debt to our environment. It won't be settled in a matter of months, and it won't be forgiven us. —*Russell E. Train (1920-)*

Let the ultimate deeds of a single person reflect that person's own true worth. —*S. M. Bertell (1951-)*

My real assets have always been acting and just being pleasant. —*Sally Field (1946-)*

Poverty is no disgrace to a man, but it is confoundedly inconvenient. —*Sydney Smith (1771–1845)*

God is my strength and power; and he maketh my way perfect. —*II Samuel 22:33*

For we brought nothing into this world, and it is certain we can carry nothing out. —*I Timothy 6:7*

When the oak is felled the whole forest echoes with its fall, but a hundred acorns are sown in silence by an unnoticed breeze. —*Thomas Carlyle (1795–1881)*

Everywhere in life the true question is, not what we have gained, but what we do.
—*Thomas Carlyle (1795–1881)*

The great and the little have need of each other. —*Thomas Fuller (1654–1734)*

I cannot say that I am the slightest degree impressed by your bigness, or your material resources. The great issue is what are you going to do with all these things? —*Thomas Huxley (1825–1895)*

As the birth of a country arises may all victory come through peace. —*Todd D. Maddocks (1969-)*

The best gift a father can give to his son is the gift of himself—his time. For material things mean little, if there is not someone to share them with. —*Unknown*

It is getting harder and harder to support the government in the manner to which it has become accustomed. —*Unknown*

When we look for the best in others, we find the best in ourselves. —*Unknown*

May all your days be filled with . . . four-leaf clovers and rainbows, smiles and laughter, and dreams come true. —*Unknown*

Courtesy is contagious. Start an epidemic. —*Unknown*

When you have nothing left but God, then for the first time you become aware that God is enough. —*Unknown*

Minds are like parachutes; they function only when they are open. —*Unknown*

Trust men and they will be true to you; treat them greatly and they will show themselves great. —*Unknown*

It's the little things that count. You can sit on top of a mountain, but you can't sit on a tack. —*Unknown*

The greatest gift I ever had came from God. I call him Dad. —*Unknown*

The world will never be the dwelling place of peace until peace is found in the heart of each and every man. —*Unknown*

Yesterday is a cancelled check. Tomorrow is a promissory note. Today is the only cash you have. Spend it wisely. —*Unknown*

You cannot buy enthusiasm. . . . You cannot buy loyalty. . . . You cannot buy the devotion of hearts, minds, or souls. You must earn these. —*Unknown*

We don't believe in miracles—we rely on them. —*Unknown*

Every man is a whole volume, just dying to be read. —*Unknown*

Some people who cast their bread upon the waters expect it to return as French toast. —*Unknown*

How well you like hard work often depends on whether you are doing it or paying for it. —*Unknown*

In order to be a true man or a true woman one needs to be committed, totally dedicated, to something bigger than oneself. —*Unknown*

We have all drunk from wells we did not dig and have been warmed by fires we did not build. —*Unknown*

Men who are occupied in the restoration of health to other men, by the joint exertion of skill and humanity, are above all the great of the earth. They even partake of divinity, since to preserve and renew is almost as noble as to create. —*Voltaire (1694–1778)*

It's kind of fun to do the impossible. —*Walt Disney (1901–1966)*

If you can dream it, you can do it. —*Walt Disney (1901–1966)*

Too many of us hear without heeding, read without responding, confess without changing, profess without practicing, worship without witnessing, and seek without sharing. —*William Arthur Ward (1921-)*

God's strength behind you, his concern for you, his love within you, and his arms beneath you are more than sufficient for the job ahead of you. —*William Arthur Ward (1921-)*

Destiny is not a matter of chance, it is a matter of choice. —*William Jennings Bryan (1860–1925)*

Frugality is good, if liberality be joined with it. The first is leaving off superfluous expenses; the last bestowing them to the benefit of others that need. The first without the last begets covetousness—the last without the first begets prodigality. —*William Penn (1644–1718)*

The biggest things are always the easiest to do because there is no competition. —*William Van Horne (1843–1915)*

Mother is the name for God on the lips and in the hearts of little children. —*William "Make peace" Thackeray (1811–1863)*

Action is eloquence. —*William Shakespeare (1564–1616)*

When people contribute to your sense of self-worth and self-esteem, they give you more than money can buy. —*Wintley Phipps (1955-)*

I hope that young people will strive to contribute not only to their own nation's welfare but to the benefit of mankind as a whole. —*Yasutaro Imai (1908-)*

I would have rather originated the Red Cross than to have written the Constitution of the United States. —*Will Rogers (1879–1935)*

INDEX

Numbers indicate page(s) on
which author is cited.

C

H

I

J

K

M

T

U

V

W

Y

Z